In the beginning

was the Word

and so shall it be again,

and the Word

is the Law,

and the Law

is Love.

A Leaders of the Way book

From the same publisher:

The Way of Love

*Joseph of Arimathea Tells the True
Story behind the Message of Christ*

Compiled by Peter Wheeler

ISBN 90-75635-01-X. 256pp

(Also available in Dutch)

The Memories of Josephes

Soul Memories of a Cousin of Jesus

David Davidson

ISBN 0-9532007-0-1. 256pp

In preparation:

The Way of Truth

Compiled by Graham Timmins

The Way of Stones

Compiled by Zanne Findlay

The Way of Diet and Health

Compiled by Rosalind Pencherek

THE CHILDREN OF LIGHT

Father Abraham on the
Fulfilment of a Prophecy

Compiled by David Davidson

Copyright © 1998 The Leaders Partnership.

Series Editor: Peter Wheeler
Copy Editor: Judith Timmins
Editorial Panel: Zanne Findlay,
Josef Schmied, Graham Timmins
Research: Daniela Pencherek and Anthony Felt

Published by The Leaders Partnership,
PO box 16457, London, SE14 5WH, UK.
ISBN 0-9532007-2-8

First edition 1998. Printed in the UK
by Redwood Books, 23 Bedford Square,
London, WC1B 3HH
Set in 11 on 14 point Galliard

Contents

The Children of Light

Introduction to the Monograph Series

The Arimathean Foundation has been established to promote and distribute the Spiritual Teachings of Joseph of Arimathea, Father Abraham and the Prophet Elijah, who currently speak through a deep-trance channel.

Our first publication, 'The Way of Love', is a biography of Joseph of Arimathea, his family, the events surrounding his life and that of his nephew Yeshua, who was to become the Christ. The second book, 'The Memories of Josephes' is an intimate account of the life of the elder son of the Arimathean who was the cousin, companion and confidant of Yeshua. In addition to major works, this series of smaller publications has been established for specific subjects from the three Spiritual Teachers as well as inspired writings from the Arimathean Group.

It is appropriate that the first in the series of these monographs should be on the Children of Light, as Father Abraham of the old Testament is the spiritual leader of these children. This publication comprises the contents of five hour-long discussions with Father Abraham. He has set out the needs, purpose and vision of a generation of very old souls who, with our help and encouragement, will restore balance, harmony and spiritual understanding to a world that is teetering on the edge of disaster.

This book is not only for the parents and guardians of these children but also for the Children of Light themselves, and for anyone who cares about the future of humanity and the planet.

Peter Wheeler, *Series Editor*

Foreword

It is a great pleasure to put in a foreword to all Children of Light, guardians and loved ones who read this book.

To be a 'Child of Light' may sound a daunting prospect. With the fear of God bred into us through the Piscean age, it may sound like a title given to a member of some strange religious cult. But this, like all other labels usually needed as an explanation or definition, is only a tool to be used in discussion. Sooner than we think these children will quickly become adults of light, and no doubt their role will be crystal clear by then.

Recently I was speaking to my wonderful auntie, a teacher with a deep spirituality, and telling her my interpretation of why these magnificent souls are returning from spirit with their finished evolution, their completed Higher Self achieved at the time of Atlantis and Egypt. She commented that she had seen this awareness in some of the children in her class. I talked about the Piscean age which we are just completing, an age where the God light, the pure white Christ light, was beginning to be reabsorbed, leading people to search for the source. Now with the Aquarian age (the crossover started in the sixties,) we have an awareness of this light within us. It is part of ourselves and our Higher Selves. The light is connecting with all life, creating all life and this light and love is constantly expanding and increasing.

Those of us born in the Piscean age may still have a long way to travel to become a complete Higher Self. Our path may meander through many more lives on earth and on different planes in spirit, but maybe we too will decide to return with our completed evolution in another two thousand years or so and teach skills we have learnt. Maybe we will also have a warm welcome, such as we need to give to these Children of Light. With this understanding we can acccept souls that have a complete connection with the God force, the Christ Light, and no longer need to be frightened of them, no longer burning them as witches, nor worshipping them as gods. We can love them and look after them so they can just BE, and respect their pure connection which will always glow within them. They have an immense love for their planet, a love which has been lost somewhere in the material age of the Pisceans.

Even though I am speaking of them being of the purest

energy, completed souls on a spiritual level, they are very much of the Earth. As you read the book you will be taken to the time of Atlantis where energies were set deep within the Earth, and these have slowly been expanding through the Piscean age, preparing for the Aquarian age. The Children of Light will instantly be part of these energies of the planet and this will bring a total balance with their spiritual connections. Much of the work that they will be drawn to will be cultivating the ground and working with animals, making all our wonderful findings and inventions environmentally friendly and securing a more organic environment. They will have the skills to improve the natural methods of living that we are discovering, for example solar and wind-powered energies to replace fossil fuels which are quickly running out. They have the ability to redis-cover the Earth's mysteries and have a great knowledge of crys-tals, which is often the first sign of a Child of Light. They will translate Egyptian texts and other manuscripts that have been hidden from the public.

So their work is very much down to earth. There should not be any fears of these children becoming overwhelmed by being special as they have no inhibitions; they know who they are and where they are going. This is a large generalisation; we must remember that all this is very deep in their beings and will come out in many forms, maybe forms we don't totally under-stand. Furthermore the fact that they are still gifted with 'free will,' and come without karma means that with the Children of Light anything is possible.

Deep down these ideas may ring true to you, and hope-fully you are constantly questioning. I have been taught by the channelled group of ascended Masters, one being Abraham, from the age of twelve, so luckily (and sometimes unluckily, but mostly luckily!) I have been aware of my spirituality and the natural connection a child has with the creative God force, his or her creator. This is a connection most people leave behind after puberty, as they enter into the material world. I feel I have been allowed a glimpse of what the Children of Light will be experiencing, and it has been said that there are a lot of fore-runners such as myself. I would like to share some of my expe-riences and feelings which I hope will help your understanding.

I went through school feeling alien, sometimes having special insights into what was being taught, but most of the time feeling awkward. I would reject the teaching as it felt patronising and demeaning. In order to survive I brought humour into the class. Luckily I was understood by my extremely spiritual mother.

If you are a Child of Light, or you know a Child of Light, you probably know how difficult it can be at school, feeling like you are wasting your time learning things that come very naturally to you. Frustrated over being so young in human years, with a soul so full of knowledge. No one wants to listen to your wonderful ideas, nor to your revelations and realisations of the world, of the stars, of your inner self, or beings you see and feel that others don't. There is a strong impatience, wanting to grow in years so you can be taken seriously. You don't constantly want to be told how special you are, although occasionally it would be nice! I remember feeling, 'I know that I'm lovely; give me something I can put this love into. I have so much work to do and so little time; don't tell me to be patient.'

This frustration is so enormous and is such a wonderful yet painful experience, it feels as if no one can comprehend the confusion. From an early age I spent most of my time within my thoughts and in my imagination, having visions of the future, absorbing and examining everything around me, from the mechanics of a collapsible chair through to the working of the human eye. Other children were asking questions not comprehending the answer. I was inspired with answers and then tried to work out the questions. Hopefully when the Children of Light experience these confusing and exciting times they will have many to share them with.

Although there is a beauty in spending a lot of time within thought and spirit, this can create an imbalance. It is very important to have a good grounding. When the lights were turned out at night, I felt the light was completely lost and would only be aware of the darker side of spirit, the lower planes of lost souls. I would constantly have nightmares and fear sleep. I didn't understand that within the stillness of night and the denseness of the darkness, light was more visible. Children need to understand the experience of separation between spirit and earth, so they don't linger in one or the other. To achieve this they need to feel the ground under their feet, touch the earth, love and respect nature especially the animals and fairies.

This confusion dealt me some bad cards. I was so conscious of lost souls that at one time it damaged my health. I was dyslexic partly due to my absent-mindedness, but this didn't matter; I could read my own writing and was commended for my stories and poetry. I felt many teachers were insulting my intelligence, cramming the little space I had left for outside information with their truth, when all I wanted was help to discover my own truth. I felt very alone and misunderstood, with a need for other children who would accept me. I did have a gift for reading people's energy and their needs. If they were searching for their truth, I would explain the different layers of consciousness trying to enlighten them and give them hope. I found myself helping and advising many ages from early on. I realize now I was developing skills of listening and allowing the flow of inspiration from my Higher Self, which I had been aware of from a very young age.

Today I hear of wonderful incidents where children shine their love and hope among all, such stories immediately put me in mind of the Children of Light. For example, a very young child is present at his brother's birth, and asks to be alone with the baby. The mother, fearing sibling rivalry, watches at the door, to witness the boy ask his baby brother, 'Tell me what God looks like, I've forgotten.' On another occasion a boy of seven comes home from school, upset with being taught things he already knows and says to his mother, 'Mummy, our head is like a camera, the eyes are the lens, our mind produces the picture and our mouth produces the photo.'

Looking at these wonderful Children of Light we realize that their souls are so wild and curious. We look into their deep intense eyes filled with knowledge, and listen to their direct stubbornness, respecting all life visible and invisible. They know they are enlightening everyone around them, holding the knowledge we never knew we had. We can look forward to a bright future.

Children of the Aquarian age, so full of light, feel our respect, understanding and love. Go forth and shine, be free, and free all that which is suppressed in man. So be it.

Tor Webster, *A forerunner of the Children of Light*

Introduction

The source of these revelations

These words are collated from transcripts of tape recordings of a deep-trance, direct-voice channel* who wishes to remain anonymous. Now in her late sixties, she started her channelling as many others do, through an attraction to the Spiritualist Church over twenty years ago. She was guided by experienced mediums, sat in development circles and practised her talent through private and group consultations. As time went by and she became more adept one particular Spiritual Teacher began to speak through her at first regularly and then exclusively. The quality of his teaching was recognised as profound and, as both he and she began to achieve recognition beyond Spiritualist circles, she built a following of people who came regularly to listen to the being who spoke through her and identified himself as 'the Master'.

About ten years ago the Master revealed that in a previous life he was Joseph of Arimathea, uncle and guardian of Jesus (known to his family as Yeshua) and in whose family tomb the body of Christ was laid after the crucifixion. He also said that he was the spokesperson for a group of souls on the causal plane and that when he spoke through the channel he was speaking with the accumulated wisdom of many lives, some of them quite well known. At about the same time he began to reveal to certain of the people who were regular visitors to the home of the channel that an aspect of their Higher Selves was also incarnate at the time of Christ and had a connection with the events of his life. Much of the information he gave at that time has now been collated and published in 'The Way of Love', compiled by Peter Wheeler.

In early 1993, in response to discussions with both the channel and the Master, one of those who had been identified by Joseph as having a role in the events surrounding Christ organised a reunion for all the others in a similar position. This

---

* A deep-trance channel is one who is literally 'entranced' by the teachers who speak through them. It is a very particular talent that takes many years to develop; to be able voluntarily to surrender to unconsciousness so that a spiritual being can speak requires an extraordinary trust. In this case the channel knows nothing about what has passed between the teacher who speaks through her and those who are listening until she is told by the audience or hears a tape-recording of the proceedings.

formed the basis for what has now become a regular retreat for a group that numbers thirty-six. In one of these early meetings the second of a trinity of teachers was introduced through the channel; this was the Prophet Elijah. The following year a third teacher was introduced: Father Abraham of the old Testament. The work of these three Teachers, all of whom are directly connected to the Christ, and the group that now surrounds them is primarily to do with earth-healing and spreading their words through the publication of books.

The Children of Light

Very soon after they began speaking through their channel the three Teachers started to talk about the Children of Light, young people who are being born whose souls have completed their rounds of incarnation. These souls have volunteered to return to Earth at this time in response to the spiritual, economic, political and environmental crises that face humanity in the transition from the Piscean to the Aquarian age.

There are two streams of Children of Light, the eldest of whom are now in their late teens and early twenties, loosely referred to by the Teachers as 'Leaders' and 'Followers'. At this time the Leaders are generally younger than the Followers. They spent their most important spiritual lives at the time of Atlantis and have not incarnated since. They have no karma and have access to the knowledge of their entire Higher Selves. In the case of most of humanity this knowledge is not readily available and is mediated through spirit guides, who are generally aspects of the Higher Self of the individual. The Leaders have the most pronounced spiritual attributes; they are the visionaries whose work it will be to find positions in society where their purpose will be recognised and appreciated.

The Followers, who have had more recent incarnations, learned much of their spiritual wisdom during the Egyptian dynasties. They are the creative individuals who will take up the call of the Leaders and build the structures and systems that will reflect the vision of the Golden age. Whether Leaders or Followers, what these young people have in common is a highly intuitive and determined nature, with eyes that betray an understanding quite beyond their years. Their deep inner knowing and sense of purpose means that they don't take kindly either to direction or to discipline. On the other hand they grow and glow in the presence of love.

Why now?

At the end of each age, approximately every two thousand years, a new Archangel steps forward to oversee the development and learning of humanity. In the current transition Uriel, who represents the purple light, is moving on and Michael, who represents the colour gold is coming into prominence. This is why the Aquarian age is often referred to as the Golden age. During the Piscean age the development and understanding of science was brought to a pinnacle and has provided humanity with power and wealth. However this scientific approach, without being balanced by a deeper understanding of the spiritual, has brought with it the seeds of its own destruction, seeds which are beginning to germinate across the planet. The first task of the Children of Light will be to address this imbalance, to restore to humanity an understanding of the laws of balance and harmony. Deep within, they know why they have come but even they cannot change the unwilling; they need to be seen, recognised and encouraged in their tasks.

At the request of several members of the group Father Abraham agreed to give five one-hour talks on the Children of Light, their purpose, their needs and how to recognise and assist them. Whilst they have great spiritual acumen they are still human children, with all the needs and vulnerabilities of children. They need help to establish themselves, to make sense of a world that has changed indescribably since they last were incarnate. This book is a verbatim account of these five talks, given in late 1997 and early 1998 to a small group made up of members of the group and the parents, grandparents and guardians of some of these children. The first two chapters and the questions and answers at the end of the book are taken from over ten years of discussions with Joseph of Arimathea, known as the Master, Father Abraham and the Prophet Elijah.

David Davidson, Summer 1998

Chapter 1

The Origins of the Children of Light

Abraham: In humbleness I come before you, my children, Shalom.

All: Shalom, Father Abraham

Abraham: It is indeed a time of great excitement that is beginning to dawn. The Children of Light, many of them are already in existence, within their souls looking forward to their tasks. Many of them are still in infancy and a little afraid of what lies before them, needing so much the hand of love from parents, teachers, guardians and friends. A large part of your work will be with these children, it is almost as if they will infiltrate into the groups, classes and into your lives. Some of you already have children within your families and you know this deep within you, or possibly Joseph has spoken with you of one or more of your children and the purpose that they have. He realizes how wonderful it would be for you to understand how it all began, why it was that these children decided that now was the time to return.

It all began at the time of Atlantis, the great length of time that the Atlanteans slaved and worked and endeavoured to change humanity into soul-searching, light-engendering people. Not all the Atlanteans by any means lifted their faces toward the light; indeed there were many that found their purpose very difficult to engender. However there were those that worked with crystal energy and worked also with the light streams as they encircled them, that were aware of powerful energies within the oceans which also helped the crystals to re-energise and to form their tasks and be part of the general understanding of that time.

The crisis of Atlantis

Wonderful things were created of crystal, the caves were full of them, even the sea bed was composed of many of these beautiful minerals and crystals. Then there was a choice that needed to be made. The wise ones who would visit Atlantis from their own sphere of light realized a time was coming when good and evil would fight for survival. They would come and speak to many groups in the same way as we ourselves are coming so to do. They would speak to the elders within the Temple, those that led the people and taught them as well as to those that had charge of some of the particularly potent crystals which were used for rituals and rites to lift the whole atmosphere into one of purpose and beauty.

There were also those that used the rituals for more darkened energies and this had to be overcome. There needed to be great energies, and these energies were mostly from the oceans themselves. There was a cave; now this cave was only visible two or three times a year, when the spring tides would be prevalent. At that time chosen groups of elders would walk into the cave, and a special ritual would take place in its depths. At that time noises akin to thunder would be heard coming from the depths. They did not understand what was taking place. The elders in the spheres of light did not consider it was auspicious to tell them, in case it brought forth fear.

Then came the time when it was realized that the time of Atlantis was drawing to its close. Somehow the work had to continue, the children growing had to understand how important they were to the continuance of the tribes that lived at that time. The elders explained to them that when the time came, there were many boats. They were to proceed to the shore, to go into those boats and in each one would be a leader that would take them away from the disaster area, to another land where they might begin again to create light and peace.

All these children had charge of particular groups of crystals; each one would adhere to a particular colour, whether blue or green or gold or deep pink, it mattered not, they accepted their task. They kept an assortment of these crystals at all times, and they became extremely aware of what was taking place in some of the groups to destroy their wonderful island. Over hundreds of years many have sought that land which disappeared under the oceans.

A great Teacher

On one of these occasions the elders from the spheres of light came in person. All these young people were bid to sit in an auditorium, to have with them one particular crystal which they could call their own. At a certain point within the ceremony they were led to the entrance to the cave. For some time this strange rumbling noise had been taking place deep within the bowels of the earth. But they were full of enthusiasm, fear did not enter into it, they were too full of excitement and they followed their leader into the cave. This cave was on many levels, lit with flares which showed them the way down, and as they went down and round, like a spiral staircase, deeper and deeper into the earth the rumble became louder. They walked for a long while until at last they were bidden to take the flares from the walls to light the path that they now descended into. The darkness was intense. There were twelve of these children. There was utter and complete silence, then they became aware of an essence of energy entering into them that they had never been aware of before. Tremendous power that surged through them; an awareness of everything that had happened to them in their present life and how every aspect of soul within their Higher Selves was giving forth the memory of how and when they had lived.

It was truly beautiful and awe inspiring, as each young person melted into the darkness and re-emerged as who they had been in a past life. They looked at each other with recognition and love by the light of their torches, so their crystals grew and magnified into pure light in their grasp. How long they were they were there, how long they entered into the sound of the universe – for their souls were indeed in the centre of the Earth – they knew not. They knew their purpose, they knew that who they now were would gradually change into who they would be when they were called by the Masters to serve again. It was as though they slept and when they awoke they were again in the auditorium on the island. The knowledge that had been imbued within them had made them centuries old, so wise, so sure of their purpose; they were beautiful to behold.

The downfall of Atlantis
It was not long before the event that caused the downfall of Atlantis occurred, and each as they were bidden went into their craft and were rowed away. The ancient Egyptians welcomed these children into their midst. Still those of the higher spheres would come and speak with them and be their rulers, and as each generation gave way to another the work continued. It changed greatly, it had to change with the time that needed a change, and many of them did not pass to spirit but regenerated their energies and their beings to continue with the enlightenment for all.

Then it was the time for them to return to the spirit

spheres, still aware that they would be called, that their great Teacher of that time Ahalem, who was eventually to be born as Abraham, would call them to their task. It seems almost impossible to imagine that such young children in the present day can have such a wealth of knowledge within their inner selves, but they have. They will not be bidden from their purpose, even those that are born to the uninitiated, to those that have never heard of them; as soon as they are mature enough they will find their way forward, to take others by the hand.

But this present time as they grow is so important. Waste not any opportunity to help them, let them speak with you, let them share what is in their souls. It is only by this action that many will truly understand that the world lies within their grasp. To God the Father, the world is His eldest son and therefore must be preserved for all time. Bear this in mind and use all the times that we have asked you for your meditation, for your visualisation, for the sound of the universe [*the Aum*] to issue forth from you, for your crystals to be charged and to be loved. We will guide you forward, at all times and in all places, we will be there.

Chapter 2

The Spiritual Leaders of the Children of Light

Abraham: I myself have elected to be the spiritual leader of the Children of Light. Now it was no mean task. Elijah was adamant that for the part that he had played in his lifetime upon the Earth he was eminently suitable to be their leader. We recalled the vision of the man Elijah, striding forth, magnificent in his height and in his energy, his personality, but so many in awe of him. He had such power, he was able through that power to create many things, some of which brought harm, others infinite good, but the harm was not in order to demean people or to make them feel inadequate; it was in the broadest sense of the word to teach them. If I said to teach them a lesson, it is the wrong connotation, therefore I say it was to teach them. They learned from that experience, they learned from the famines, from the droughts, from the forest fires and from the pestilence and disease, and that has always been the way of humankind – they have never appreciated what they had until they were near to losing it, and often the only way back, in order to preserve it, was some kind of pain or some kind of loss. Elijah was magnificent at this; he always warned, his hands rose in the air above him, his voice trumpeted around the distance where people stood to listen. Those in their palaces trembled: 'Elijah approaches, and what is in his wake?' Not, we felt, quite the type of leadership for young, innocent children, embarking on a life preordained to a large extent, certainly one where leadership of the gentlest kind has been envisioned. So Elijah withdrew from the battle.

Master Joseph felt a lot of his task was in gently coercing people, helping them to understand their failings and how to make them their strengths. He himself, the true teacher of experience, wished to continue not just with his little flock represented by yourselves but also the group work, those being brought in through their desire to learn, and often their curiosity and great love for these Children – many of whom had their first experience of speaking with spirit by speaking with him – and we all appreciated his desire to continue with his work.

Yeshua, the natural leader of the Children of Light is constantly within their auras, within their souls, in His extremely spiritual way of leading, but He also has not been able to come forward to any great extent because of the role that Man has placed around Him, that rather religious role that is apportioned by the Churches. Of course He will give His leadership, and as time passes, much more openly. We visualise, as the Children become more conscious of their role, that Yeshua will indeed appear and speak with them. But that is not for the immediate future, it is a little way ahead – and of course amongst your Spiritual Teachers that only left myself.

I was a little cunning over this, and that also was much of my role when I lived upon the Earth. Many said: 'Abraham lives by his wits', and many of them were right. People would come and they would lay their burdens before me, asking for my wisdom to help them to overcome whatever that burden was, and I had to be a little astute. Usually I knew the person very well, because they were within my area, often within my own community, but there were times when people would come from afar. I knew that they were travelling, word would come that someone was en route to ask about a great tragedy in their area, and hoped that with my communication with God that I could cast a little light upon it. So I did my homework and I made it my business to find out what their problem was, thus when they came and when I gave audience, as it was said, I was prepared. Not only were they surprised at my knowledge of their predicament, but that I had already communed with God and I had an answer for them. So I applied that principle in part by allowing the others to discuss their merits and demerits, and sat quietly aside until my moment to step forward arrived.

The importance of love
But there is more to leading the Children of Light than speaking with them occasionally and awaking their souls to their purpose. As in the days when I lived in flesh, I had to bear witness in principle; so also do those that lead them in the here and now have to be aware that they learn by what is presented to them. They learn by the experience of those who are older, but also by their wisdom and by their love. Without love the world would have ceased to exist a very long time ago. It was the emotion, the love, the sympathy that enabled Man to propagate, to continuously supply his Earth with that which would bear witness to God. So I do ask you at this time to be aware that as these Children come into your proximity, that you realize you do truly have a responsibility to them, especially to

those with less knowledge, less understanding of the spiritual truths. You may feel that throughout the years you have been learning not a great deal has truly been absorbed. Inadequacy flows freely amongst groups of those that are seeking truth. But it is not so much that which is on the surface that can be easily recalled and discussed as that which lies deep within the consciousness that can come forth in times of need. When others need that wisdom it flows, and these children, set apart by their very nature, their very wisdom and gentleness that they cannot comprehend, need the same approach from others that will lead them forward.

Reverting back to the Children of Light, you do all have a responsibility toward them, even if they just cross the horizon in front of you. A glance of love, a touch of understanding recognising their difficulties, is often all that is needed. With others a more direct approach, taking the teaching, sharing it with them in a very simple way, allowing them to recognise the difference between a teaching of light and a teaching of pure discipline. Both are needed, but both need that touch of lightness within them that helps that child within its understanding.

They will not always be children, they will grow with great speed into the maturity that we envision, so let their childhood be one of progress and happiness, and not one of fear. It is not all work, they may kick a ball and enjoy that as much as sitting and listening to a teacher advising them. It is both sides of their nature. Allow a child to think as a child and allow an adult the wisdom to choose.

A little further ahead, the changes within the world will begin to harmonise. Governments will change. We have spoken of this with the Children of Light. Some of them are already older, some of them, the forerunners, are the age of our son here [*a young man of twenty-one years*] and a little older than that also. They make their feelings felt, they enter into Government and into the spiritual teachings. So there is much that lies ahead, but you will not find it, any of you, if you look down there. You will only find it by looking ahead and up.

Chapter 3

Talk One, October

Abraham: My children, I embrace you. Shalom.

All: Shalom, Father Abraham.

Abraham: This is a time that has been looked forward to for a very long time. To be able to speak with each of you in this manner, to reassure you in many ways of the difficulties which might occur regarding these special children, to raise your spirits towards their advent and the changes that they will and indeed are bringing with them. But of course, as with so many things in life, any change brings a problem and the anticipation of such radical changes as those that we have all spoken of for so long does bring trepidation into the hearts of those that will be responsible for carrying many of them through.

Spreading the word
Where the Children of Light are concerned, do remember that there are millions of people throughout the world that have never even heard of them. Of course, they are aware of different energies and realize that something is taking place within their lives, but as to exactly what this is they cannot determine. Those that have such children born to them have to accept the difference in these children's natures to their own, on a different level of understanding.

Generally those within the Western world have a different kind of understanding, of awareness, of these differences within the children. Perhaps the grapevine is a little different in the way these stories are told. Perhaps some of them are aware of the ancient teachings and prophecies which bring about that anticipation at this time. But those that live in far-off countries, many of which are indeed rather primitive, it is with these that primarily I ask that you try and share your knowledge.

It is very difficult when you are sitting in your home in an advanced country to even consider how difficult it is for those who are living perhaps in a tent or in a straw dwelling or even those that have no home at all to be able to accept that children even in their infancy will make a great difference to the way that they will live. Many will come to you in the normal progression of life. You will meet them in society. You may know those that will travel great distances in order to help others to accept the change in their role. So it is not only to talk to others that you know have such children, or awareness of them, but also to those to whom it is all completely new.

Spirit and life

Some of you that are present have children already that show signs of being more advanced spiritually and have a different awareness of life itself. Many of those children may, of course, even be telling you what to do at this time. There are also those that are teaching them, that are looking for those little differences in the way that they are. But there are also those present that do not yet have them within their families nor yet are responsible for their welfare, it makes no difference. They still expect that you will share, and go out of your way to share.

Those to whom we speak within Master Joseph's combined group of Spiritual Teachers realize that the kind of knowledge that we impart has its own special responsibility, which arises within the self and which determines the future in a very different way. So I am asking each one of you on this first occasion of speaking in this way to look very hard at your sense of responsibility, your sense of intuition, your sense of guidance and to be very sure within yourselves as to your knowledge and how you are gaining it, how accurate your feelings are and from what source you gain your knowledge.

A great deal of nonsense has been spoken about the Children of Light but also a great deal of truth. I have personally spoken of the source of these children, going back as far as the time of Atlantis, shortly before the end, who were given a special power through crystals so that their minds evoked and accepted the tasks of many, many thousands of years ahead.

You see, it was already at that time known that there would be an age where it would be very necessary for the evil that had been wrought and also the incompetence that had taken place in the leadership of man to be revoked. Those children and others similar to them – for their strain continued through much of the early Egyptian dynasties – continued to absorb the knowledge of the future.

No doubt in your reading and studies you have been aware of some of the activities within the Egyptian ages. How there were those that were initiates into the planes of light, how with due care and attention from those that tended to them, their soul left the body, sometimes for weeks on end, travelled the spheres of light, received teaching about the immediate future and whether there would be invasions or whether there would be famine or drought and all the domestic situations that people worry about constantly. They were also allowed into the temples of enlightenment, so that they might scan what would take place through the actions of man which would create certain things in the future which could not be changed.

Temples of learning
The free will of man only works to a certain extent by the co-operation of humankind. Beyond that there is a way of living ordained through the principle of creation, the principle of the worlds of light within the universe and of course all the peoples of the Earth and the way that they grow, mentally and physically. So that which lay within the far future was gleaned through the spiritual awareness of the teaching within those temples. There were many that were the initiates who also realized that when their souls permanently left their bodies, that they would travel to a particular sphere where their tuition, their learning would continue, that they would indeed be called upon to return to the Earth in order to perform their tasks. Not only, of course, the Egyptian dynasties but many other places within the world where people congregated together and where they became very knowledgeable within the archaic teachings, through the mind, through meditation and also through the ability to leave their bodies for long periods of time.

The great sages
There have always been these sages that have worked hard at this progression – comparatively few to the masses within the world that have vision, but very important for their sense of direction and teaching to others. Those such as Babaji, who the Master has spoken of many times in connection with Yeshua. [*Yeshua travelled to India before his ministry began and met a great teacher known as Babaji. The full story is recounted in 'The Way of Love'.*] There have been races of men, many who have taken on the skin and race of the Indian tribes, the American Indian tribes. We have been asked on some occasions as to why they always appear to be advanced spiritually among the races of man. This is, of course, because they are so close to the earth and it is the vibration coming from the centre of the earth,

enfolding them and lifting their spirit toward the spheres of light where they have been able to form a triangle of energy which has enabled them to assist many in a far more spiritual path than Western man, with his different priorities, has been able to achieve.

This is just a little of the background of these children and their progression through many centuries, some thousands of years before that time came when many of the races virtually became extinct. They changed so much, their progression took a different angle, often a different lightstream [*see appendix*], so that that which they had been pursuing was completed and a different pursuance of teaching and enlightenment took place.

So what happened then? Most of them remained in that sphere where they would continue their form of enlightenment, simply awaiting the passing of time until it was apposite to return to the Earth and commence their ministry. If you look upon these children as the ministers of light, you will be very close to what they must achieve. We always look upon ministers, do we not, as those with a greater spiritual energy and knowledge that we can go to in order to help us in times of need. So these children as they grow will no longer be infants, no longer coming into the tortures of adolescence, as all young people must indeed do. But they will be able to turn on that special inner consciousness and in that manner, however young they may be in years, they will be old in memory and in opportunity to help.

The role of the Children of Light

As they become older, what truly is their role? How can we recognize within these children that particular quality which will be so important to the furtherance of man's ability to live upon his Earth and care for his Earth?

Initially when they are born they react in a different way to those around them. It is as though they are tuning in to an energy which is higher than that of the room where the birth takes place. Even their first cry into life is less anguished and more contained, even joyous, than those who come into life in the normal method of progression. And when they open their eyes, they look around, they perceive the changes that have taken place since their last emergence into the world.

These children have one different awareness of life to the general birth pattern of infancy. The great majority of them are souls returning, not aspects within the Higher Self but the Higher Self *per se* that are coming into life. Not all of them are the true Leaders. Many of them will be there to do the bidding of the Leaders among them, to see the wisdom of new laws, and to help them to instigate these laws. And these children, the Followers, while still of generations of the special awareness coming down, as we have described, are aspects within a Higher Self that lived at a time when their main knowledge, their main attention to the detail of the future was taking place. If this were not so, they would not be able to function as Children of Light. There is virtually no one that can take them back to the time of that tuition, the time of that instigation, initiation, into their tasks.

The isolation of the Children of Light

Every one of you that are here are aspects within a Higher Self. How can you possibly know the isolation that many of these children feel? With a wealth of knowledge deep within them, such a longing to share and yet because of their inexperience within their bodies they have to be like all children, obedient to those that care for them, those that teach them. In no way can they stand up and say to their teacher, 'But you are wrong. The way that you teach geography is not the way that we know geography,' and this applies to all other teachings that are learnt in school. Many of those things they will be taught, they will simply shrug off and put into a compartment of useless information. Instead they will turn to those things which will be very important to them: the movement of the planets in the sky, the birth of new stars, knowing the part that they will play within Earth's life, knowing that many of these stars, still millions of miles distant from the sight of the astronomers, will have an energy that will change the tides, the patterns of the weather, and even the way that the Earth vibrates and man is able to relate to his Earth.

Awareness of the past and future

They will also pay far more attention to the insight within them. They will have a very special awareness of events, events of the past and events yet to come. You may well know of children in your care who have asked you to heed warnings that they are giving, warnings of difficulties that you will encounter, and you will do well to heed them. Those who, by tuning in to the energies of progress, will see potential warfare, uprisings, dissension within countries, civil wars. We have been aware of those children who in their minds have approached us, as your Teachers, so aware of carnage in an area of the world where there will be eruptions within mountains, landslides, terrible earthquakes. 'No one will listen to us,' they say. 'Can you tell them and warn them?' In their sleep state they do indeed travel. They travel to planes of light far, far more distant than your souls are able to do. You go to some of the planes where you are able to have conversation with loved ones that have gone on before, teachers that you know are close to you, aspects of your Higher Selves that have learned wisdom and wish to share it. You do not always have a clear recognition, but you do go there. Some of those among you travel to places where there have been recent disasters, either helping souls to recover from loss or damage or taking some of the souls that have passed in the tragedy through the doorway of light where there are those waiting to receive them. All these are tasks that you do, my children, as spiritually enlightened and growing people, but the Children of Light do far, far more. When they return from travelling to a distant sphere, they long to be able to share it.

Autism

Some of these children are autistic. They cannot share because their pattern of thought prohibits speech, but it doesn't mean that they are stupid, that they are idiots – far, far from this. So they are unable to control the movement of their bodies but this is because for hundreds and thousands of years they have had no bodies. Can you imagine that if you were one of those that go up in a spacecraft, are you going to walk out of it and remain steady on your feet? And that might only be for a few months. They need very special understanding. There are those among you who might desire to learn how to help them to break through that barrier that they find distressful as well as those who have given birth.

Abortion

And talking of giving birth, as science has progressed it is alarming to your Teachers that there is now the acceptance within the fraternity of medicine to end the lives of children who are found, using ultrasound, to have these problems and a termination is recommended. We applaud those who say, 'But I want my child. I love my child and will help my child to overcome.' For each child has its purpose; some of them are brilliant within their knowledge and they can express it in their own way as they grow. Musically, perhaps, or by the use of modern, up-to-date equipment, they can find voice through it and a use for their fingers or even their toes. Nature takes care of those embryos that cannot face life. So we ourselves disapprove, we fear greatly the progression of medicine that will allow healthy children to be terminated because they appear to be mentally insufficient within their abilities.

Unfortunately we have no say, but you have say. You can spread enlightenment through your family doctor, through a doctor that you might be friends with, through those that have life and death in the palms of their hands. It is these responsibilities, beloved children, that we place upon your shoulders. Those of you who feel you are inadequate, that you cannot speak for nations, then we ask, or tell, you that what we will be saying in the next few sessions is not for you.

In order that we may answer some of your questions this day, I will not continue with an exposé about the children. We will talk more on their role and how to recognize them when next we are together. What I will do first is to seat myself comfortably so that I may listen to your words and reply in the way I feel necessary.

Do please speak, my children.

Q: Do dyslexia and the Children of Light go hand in hand?

A: Not altogether. Dyslexia has been a difficulty over many generations but it does usually mask the ability to relate mentally and often physically, between those children and the world in which they find themselves. Very often children born with that condition, or who develop it very quickly after birth, are those whose souls have not allowed an aspect to come to the earth for a very long time.

It is not all souls that release aspects on a regular basis. Some may feel that every 2,000 years at the commencement of an age is sufficient for the kind of knowledge that it wishes to absorb, while others are eager for life and eager for knowledge and release many aspects virtually at the same time throughout the world in order to glean that awareness. There is no fixed rule but we have found that because of the long sojourn in their

sphere of light there are an unusual number who are born with
this difficulty.

*Q: Where there is a Child of Light and both parents refuse to
accept any spiritual understanding, how is the situation best dealt
with, especially when the child is conscious that it is a Child of
Light and knows its work and its light? Is it the child that is going
to make the parents understand or is it others that have got to try
and teach these parents?*

A: Each child of course has its own motivation, its own purpose
in life as well as the united purpose of the future. It also has the
soul purpose which it needs to recognize and sometimes come
to terms with. It is often a great awakening to the parents as
they are forced to recognize that their child is a little different,
either from their earlier children or from the children of friends.
If you see that there is a real difficulty taking place between
child and parents, then watch that family's progress and either
you yourself or others who are there to help, keep an eye on the
growing child, be there so that when they need help, when they
need someone to speak to who will really understand their
predicament, their dilemma, that you can provide it for them.

*Q: You said the children are forced to learn subjects in particular
ways and they know that that's not the correct way. When you have
children and these children have to follow a format set down by the
Government of the day, how can you teach them, and how can you
make them do otherwise?*

A: This is where their home environment has its place and is so
important. With a caring understanding parent this obstacle can
be very largely, if not removed, then set aside. You can explain
to your child that certain things must be done in life not for
pleasure but because it is accepted and is laid down in law. That
as they grow older they will gain the benefit from the knowledge of things that do not particularly interest them at the
moment, but may be very important for them to know when
they are mature. So there is that form of help for the child and
there is also, if they are in a school that is particularly unaware
of their needs – because many of them will have an unusual
interest in crystals, for example, or in colour, or in light, or in
the astronomy area of knowledge which the school might not

initially provide – these activities can take place outside of the school hours, possibly during the time of the holidays.

Always be aware – and this applies to all present – that things are changing very rapidly. Governments are finding that rules are not set in stone. As people progress, as they become more understanding of the spiritual and of their basic needs and what will help them to live, the rules have to be changed. Schooling patterns now are vastly different from even fifty years ago; certainly the last century's educational pattern is the reverse of what is taking place now. So these gradual changes are helpful to the environment and to the ability that these children have. The more of these children that are born and live through the first few years of life and go to school, the more the changes will take place as they demand certain items within the curriculum and even guide the teachers toward providing what they want.

Q: I understand the difficulty of having the foetus aborted because of something that the scan shows is not right and that this is preventing the facet of The Higher Self being born, but have they not the chance to come again at a later time or would it be a completely different facet of the Higher Self which comes the next time?

A: These children do have the availability of future life. With other children, as you know from the teaching [*see appendix*], that facet returns to the Higher Self, shares its little bit of experience and remains as part of the whole, while another aspect may come back to the same parents, if they are suitable, depending on why these people had chosen the abortion of course, or maybe to different parents, again accordingly. But the Children of Light, the Leaders among them, the ministers among them, they can return and try again and try to ensure, as they all do, that there is sufficient perfection in the embryo to allow the continuance of the pregnancy and not to produce things that really fail society and encourage the abortion.

They do not decide to be dyslexic, blind, deaf, dumb from choice. It is because of their inexperience and their long sojourn in spirit that produces this. They will overcome it and possibly in a generation or so, they will be as bright and as able to live up to their reputation as all other children that survive the act of birth.

Q: Is there a special way to bring up these children and should we remove from them certain influences, such as television and other things like this?

A: Indeed not, to your last comment, because this is part of their present, this is part of the life that enfolds them in the now. If you remove these things they will be at a disadvantage with their peers who will consider them to be old-fashioned little beings, which can make them very sad. It can even make them angry and resentful, and we do not want this. They should be encouraged to do the same things as the children they are learning with and playing with. In their own way they can bring their specialized knowledge into the life of those children, thus sharing the responsibility with many others that will have to live with them in adulthood, will have to be part of the workforce that they are endeavouring to lead, to change the way of life so that it is happier and better for them.

They can also bring into the environment the necessary changes through their greater knowledge that is needed with these modern things, for example, computers. It is not generally recognized, although medicine is beginning to understand more clearly the effects of radiation of human beings, that until fairly recently people could sit for hours in front of a screen and not realize the damage being done to the cells in their body. It should indeed be possibly for two hours, then move away, do other things, get some fresh air, have a meal, whatever other things you need to do in your day; then have another brief period of time before that screen. The terrible wave of tiredness in industry is largely the blame of this kind of equipment.

Other illnesses, such as motor neurone disease, have their root cause in modern times, because of addiction to the screens, either sitting too close to a television screen or in a cramped environment without sufficient fresh air before a computer. We hope that some of these children will become scientists and will perfect a way that special screens can be placed in front of the radiation that will prevent people from forming illnesses of the nervous system. It doesn't so much affect the essential organs and the way that they must work. It is the nervous system that is greatly affected and when that is affected it also affects the brain. So do heed this word of warning, and also it is particularly vital that women who are pregnant stay away from computers because it affects the child as well as themselves.

We now feel that our time with you on this occasion is complete and we had better say farewell, all of us who are here surrounding me at this time, all eager to learn, (you would think that they had enough time, wouldn't you, to learn these things?). Everyone wishes to say farewell to you all and hope to see the same auras next time that we come and speak with you, with lots of questions and lots of interest. So now, may love shower upon you, restoring your energies and allowing your light to indeed shine forth. Shalom.

All: Shalom.

Chapter 4

Talk Two, November

Abraham: My children, blessings to you. Shalom.

All: Shalom, Father Abraham.

Abraham: So time has past and again we are here to discuss what is occurring within the universe regarding the Children of Light. But before I continue along my chosen ideas I wish first to have a briefing, as it were, as to any questions that have arisen from my last talk with you. Maybe there are a few points that you wish to argue with, or that you have not completely understood. Now this little exercise is not for discussing the children of your knowledge or within your family. It is indeed to discuss the content of our talk last time. So we will give a little while to this and then I will continue with my theme. So who wishes to speak first?

Q: What percentage of children are Children of Light?

A: We would say possibly one percent of the world population will be a Child of Light when all of them have incarnated upon the Earth. It will be, we would say, two generations, possibly another twenty-five or thirty years before the main flow have ceased to incarnate. Between now and then there will be an acceleration of youth that we would name Children of Light.

Q: You spoke of the original twelve of these children going into the centre of the earth. I imagine these were very exceptional children. Are they children yet to be born or are they already born?

A: Those particular children will not be born into the world for that function. They were the originators. They were even those that were the origin of the twelve tribes. It was from each of these that a tribe was initiated [*the twelve tribes of Israel*] So they are now within the spirit realm, watching the progress of these children as it takes place, guiding them mentally and on a soul principle, but no, they will not themselves come into flesh. A good point that, my child.

Q: Will they guide, through channelling?

A: We do not feel that that is particularly likely to happen. It is not considered now, but nothing is ruled out because as soon as the children are born they come under the same auspices as all other children with their awareness of free will. No one can be quite sure as to the pattern of life these children will follow. They will have access to a remarkable amount of knowledge because they are the equivalent of their complete Higher Selves. We will mention a little more of this for those of you that were not here before or are not really very sure about what is entailed within the Higher Self. But those that need a specific form of energy to channel through them will indeed be able to find that. There is always a source of teaching which all of humanity, whatever their purpose, is able to reach and to obtain enlightenment from, but whether it will be from those twelve we doubt very much indeed.

The Higher Self
Before we ask for another question, may we speak just for a few minutes, reiterating what we often tell people who come for the first or second time to hear of our truth, our wisdom regarding the Higher Self, because it is well worth reiterating for a book. Many people when they apply themselves to presenting a book often keep very closely to the channelled words. They do not always realize that many of those that will ultimately read that book may not be aware of some of the finer points of general teaching and they may be bewildered when they hear such statements as 'The Children of Light are their own Higher Selves'. There will be those that might well say, 'What is a Higher Self and are these Children of Light not quite human?'

Basically the Higher Self is the total soul. It is that part of soul that was shattered into millions of atoms at the time during Creation when the world was completed and when the intelligent life was being formed to populate the Earth. As near as we are able to advise you, that would be at the time of the first individual human beings that were born after the Els had returned to the spirit realms [*see page 84*], deciding that their function of travelling between the spheres of light and the Earth had been completed. They left behind a species of man that had arrived through their own inter-reaction with Earth people.

So there were those upon the Earth that were still very primitive but there were also those that were part of these Elders of spirit who had a great awareness of spiritual matters, but not so much the reasoning ability to divide the spiritual from the secular. Like those who are predominantly in the spirit spheres, they had no way of decision-making, of deciding whether or not they would be able to make plan A or plan B, to remember the past or to go forward to the future and to use a gift which had not yet been bestowed upon them, which was the gift of free will, of a dual purpose within their lives to which they could choose to belong. So it was that the massive explosion of soul took place and all these atoms were then available to be drawn into humanity, providing a link between God and man, allowing the intelligence to develop and grow and to allow also that this wonderful gift of free will could be accepted and with that, intelligence could be used.

Old and new souls

There was much at that time that was not absorbed into individual man. The population of the world was relatively small, especially in comparison with today. Now many people have asked us, 'What is a new soul, what is an old soul?' To be clear on this, I would say that an old soul is one which at the beginning of this time began to be associated with that atom which comprised the Higher Self, splitting itself into countless atoms within the whole. So each life ultimately to be lived would have its own ability to choose the path within that life, the ability to have the past shared with it before entering into its life, and the ability, when that life was completed, to share the experience with all other atoms within that whole. Those atoms of soul that were not at that time able to find a host in which they could live remained to a large extent within the universe and, as the population increased, became much greater. As different species were born, as certain animal species became more intelligent and gradually developed into more primitive humankind, so the opportunity of those atoms to enter into such beings took place. Therefore those who are born into life, who some people feel are a little primitive, a little without a great deal of intelligence, are referred to as a new soul. They know very little about the principles of life, about spiritual aspects of development. So this is the best comparison that we are able to give. There may at sometime be a further teaching that one of us will be able to give, either to an individual or to a group that will throw more light upon it, but of course we do not wish the whole session to be taken up on the subject. It is just so that those who are not so well acquainted with the principle may be able to think about it and to learn more about why man is here and how the growth takes place [*see also appendix*].

Now we are open again to questions, even a question on that, if you wish.

Q: I think in your last talk you said that the pure Children of Light were their complete Higher Selves, whereas the other Children were not. Could you just confirm that?

A: That is correct. The Leaders of the Children of Light are their total Higher Selves. They are those that will become the leaders of society. They are those that with their great knowledge of what is required of them throughout the Aquarian or Golden age will find many others that will follow them who can be, as it were, their spokesmen in countless areas for the truths that will come naturally from within themselves. Now those children, the Followers, they very well may need further instruction and guidance from within their Higher Selves in order to be able to function in the best possible way. But the pure Children are those from the age of Atlantis, those who since then have been imbibing pure knowledge on how to resurrect a dying world, how to dispense with the evil, with the destruction, albeit over a long period of time – it has taken all this time for the world to reach its present stage, let alone to recover from it. The Followers will need direction far more than the pure Children of Light and it is very possible that those of you who are here who are aware of the special needs of these children may not be quite sure as to which child is a pure Child of Light and which is a Follower so we do intend to help you to understand this a little more.

Any more questions?

Q: A question about the twelve again. Am I right in thinking that their energies went into the crystals that are still in the centre of the earth, in that cave?

A: It was combined in a way that the energies would be very fluid between the human aspect which also contained its own crystalline structure and that of the crystals that were manifest then, so that many of those crystals, the purity of them, had an intelligence which other crystals might not yet have acquired.

Now there are certain crystals which people are attracted to where they feel immediately that there is an energy within them to which they can relate. They feel as though the crystals are speaking with them, directing them, stopping them from making foolish choices, protecting them and so forth. And these crystals could very well be particles, pieces of the original that have become detached from the parent crystal [*from Atlantis*] and that thereby have found their way into many homes. The actual crystals that were worked on, and with, by those twelve children we do not feel will ever be found by man and used by them in the simple way that most people are able to use their crystals because those crystals are an integral part of the Earth harmony, the Earth energy and vibration.

The Earth has its own crystalline structure which is echoed within mankind; it is thereby possible for man and Earth to inter-relate together. The Earth has to have its power source; it cannot simply exist within the universe without that to which it adheres. So those particular crystals would be reabsorbed into the Earth structure and be a very important part of its ability to regenerate, to help the emotions of man to change, to become less selfish, to be more motivated toward helping each other, toward the emotion of love, rather than the primitive and very unhappy emotion of hate and destruction.

Q: Are there Children of Light and Children of Darkness and could this lead to conflict in the future?

A: Not war as most people consider it to be. Not a taking-up of arms with physical destruction. It is more a battle of wills. It will be that of divine power and knowledge against ignorance and fear. Fear is a very primitive emotion, it is bestowed upon man so that mankind can be aware of his mortality. The original knowing of fear was to prevent tragedies such as being eaten by animals or walking off the edge of a cliff or some other dangerous occupation, not realizing perhaps that destruction would thus follow. So the energy of fear was a warning, it was that which man would react to in certain situations. But it has, of course, developed into something much greater than this. It has developed into an emotion which encourages man to fight back, to destroy that which has given rise to the fear instead of using that emotion to help the self to be able to help others to a more spiritual understanding and trust. It is used in all these negative and very horrific ways. Fear of occupation, fear of loss, fear of dying, fear of health being destroyed – these are more primitive aspects of fear but very important to humanity.

The Children of Light will be able to use the fear aspect in a different way. There will be a greater perspective of how they can control their lives, what they are able to do and what they should refrain from doing. Their main problem is going to be the part played by their guardians. We use this word instead of always having to refer to parents, teachers, guardians and so forth. We will in future simply say 'the guardian of the child'.

Explaining to the Children
Now many guardians, because of their own upbringing, their own feelings within them of wishing to nurture their child, to prevent accidents – especially at this time with the horrific incidences of evil in bringing the children into the clutches of those that wish to damage them in one way or another – will put an embargo on to many of the things that these children feel they should experience and should help their growth.

We are not saying that you should allow your child unlimited experience at a very young age. What we are saying is, it should be explained to them the dangers that are around them, exactly what is taking place, how careful they should be with their reaction and inter-reaction with human beings they do not know, how to take responsibility for themselves, and if you are really sure that your child is a Child of Light, to allow the intelligence, the awareness within that child to accept her or his responsibility.

Encouraging responsibility
While very young, do take all the care that you would with any young child in your care, but as they grow older, become more responsible and better able to take care of themselves, then foster this within them. Allow them to understand their purpose, to read the material that has been written. There will be a response which will come from deep within. If there is no response, you have misdiagnosed your child.

You might very well have a child that is an assistant [*a follower*], is one that knows the purpose is to bring spiritual peace, light, beauty, relief from pain, fear, all these other aspects within people's lives. Most of them will be very gentle. You will have the healers, those that care for young children, for animals, the old, the infirm. These are the active members of youth, who realize their own role, their own ability, who will no doubt argue with you if your way of thought is different from theirs. They are not as assertive as the pure Children of Light, who know the way they are going and woe betide anybody who endeavors to stop them!

Even when very young there will be certain ways that you can be reasonably sure that your child is what you feel he or she is. There is no predominance of male or female. There is a total balance of energies but it does not even mean that two Children of Light may form an alliance or may wish to marry or live together. They are more likely to choose a companion from one of the Followers, the helpers, than one of their own kind. They are so infinitely bossy that relationships with each other would be a constant battleground. But this is in years to come. Quite a few of the Followers of the Children of Light are older than they are. They could be in their 20s, born in order to lead the way, to have an awareness of the need of the Earth, of the moving into a spiritual sphere and leaving behind the recognized religions that dominate so greatly within the world. So as the centuries pass, this will become an archive of memory which people will respond to in their own way, possibly being amazed that man for a whole age could have been so ignorant of truth, should have followed so blindly a very narrow pathway that did not liberate, it enchained man into a narrow mode of thought and activity.

Those older children are invaluable in their input toward these pure Children of Light. They recognize what is taking place within them. Many are teachers and those teachers who are trained in any case to see the value of certain qualities within children and to encourage them will soon see that certain children will not follow the norm. They will not simply learn as they are shepherded into different classes with different ways of presenting knowledge.

Highly individual

So the Children of Light themselves are highly individual as they grow into adults, and will be the true leaders. They will be in charge of governments, in charge of the spiritual centres. They will be the surgeons of the future, using more natural methods because surgery will become a method to use when all else has failed. The alternative medicines and those that complement other more stringent ways of curing illness – it is these things that the Children of Light will be responsible for. Because they have this knowledge of the ancient past, those things that took place in Atlantis, especially with crystals, these will be used by them and they will be able to institute their colleges, sciences and all else that is important for man to gradually live by. Their evolution depends upon it because without this the present species of mankind will simply die out. In another hundred years there will be very few upon the Earth that can tolerate the pollution, the overcrowding and the severely limiting ways of society. This is why the Children of Light have come at this time. They will provide the means to insist that the way of mankind changes and the methods they will use will not be subtle.

At this point, any more questions?

Q: Could I ask, is there any risk that these children will fall into the way of drugs?

That is an excellent question to ask us. Because they have an inquiring mind and they will want to know all the pros and cons of a situation, it is quite likely that they will dabble in – what is it called? – the drugs scene, but in a different way. Not simply to obtain sensation which cannot be obtained through normal way of living, but to be able to ascertain how it can be used in order to help society, help man to overcome certain illnesses, to promote more health by using the drug in a constructive way. So they are not those that will unfortunately become – hooked, shall we say? – upon these drugs and encourage other people to partake in them.

Experimentation rather than addiction
If they take drugs it will be rather more as an experiment and in so doing, make notes, be it scientific or chemical, their own feelings within them as they take minute quantities, and they will learn by what is occurring. Of course, all parents who realize that their children are experimenting in this way should indeed speak with them upon what they are embarking on. We are sure that those that are the guardians of the Children of Light will be reassured by what they are told. But those guardians and parents that are particularly against the imbibing of drugs, be it the hard drugs of the present time, be it ciga-

rettes, alcohol or even pain-killers which are meant to alleviate pain should be aware that when these are taken in great abundance, because there is no other way to alleviate the pain, then this also becomes a habit that is difficult to break. The whole scenario is one born of stress, stress within an uncaring world, a world that simply wishes to throw the responsibility of man in a different direction.

So as they understand more about drugs, about alternatives and complementary things, the whole scenario will change and people will predominate who care for others and not simply wish to destroy them.

Q: Will illegal drugs be used by the Children of Light and will they be able to show that there are positive effects, that drugs can be used to enlighten?

A: Initially, yes they will. However, we would argue with you a little about part of your statement, that drugs can be used to enlighten. The only enlightenment that we can see is under very careful experiment, in a laboratory with fully trained medical and scientific people, the chemists of the present and the future, who can monitor the effects of all manner of drugs on carefully chosen people who wish to help medicine, help society to overcome the habit of the present.

Those who experiment, however carefully they feel they are doing this, are not realizing most of the time the danger they are in, because experimentation with any kind of drug which affects the nervous system can become one which they cannot move away from. They get deeper and deeper into the mire, needing stronger and stronger drugs in order to promote sanity in between their travels and of course in the end there is no sanity, there is no ability to overcome, the body breaks down with all its organs becoming saturated within the drug and then the young – or the old – they die more from the effect of the large amount of drugs they are taking than from the illness or the illusions that they are trying to escape from. Most of the drug-taking when it comes to cannabis and similar drugs are taken because of boredom and the other stronger medical drugs are taken because there is no peace of mind to use natural methods to overcome pain and illness.

Q: Seeing the impact of free will on mankind today, can the parents of the Children of Light be assured that the Children of Light will not make the wrong choice because of their freedom of will in any aspect of their lives?

A: No one can be that sure, we wish they could be. It is indeed a rather biased gift. It is the equivalent of giving your child a firearm and also giving him the bullets to place within it and trusting that common sense will prevent him from putting the two together and firing it. He might well realize that he has in his hands a weapon of destruction but he may not use his free will to lay it aside so we cannot be that categoric as to whether or not these children will use their gift always in the best possible way. However, when the Children of Light and their Followers cohere together, discuss together, relate their intentions, then a more perfect balance begins to emerge.

So many people find that they have one of each within their families. The Child of Light chooses their guardian; they will often also choose a sibling that they can relate to and can create the harmony of atmosphere and peace around them that they need for their own progression. So you will find many households that have two children that when very small will seem to constantly argue and fight, but as they grow a little older they reach a harmony together and they complement each other in quite a different way.

Q: I am extremely interested in the role of the guardians. Could you say more about this?

A: We can speak a little more. Very often Master Joseph has spoken upon the role of parents chosen by souls in the karmic pattern of living, and this is a very similar situation, except of course that the Leaders of the Children of Light have no karma so there is nothing that comes into life with them that they have to overcome, learn from and progress through. So this is one of the ways that you might be able to ascertain more clearly if the child that you would consider as a Child of Light is indeed such. The Children of Light choose even more carefully the parents they are to be born to. They might be born to a single parent, realizing that what they need to learn and overcome within their lives is more applicable to being with one lone parent, struggling to keep them, love them, provide for them than they would have in a secure home with both parents, affluence and plenty. Most of these young people will disregard what is happening around them because of what they know their purpose is to be. So they choose the guardian in order that they may inter-relate with both or one of those guardians, realizing that there is knowledge already within the being of the parent which might not be in another member of the family or in another member of society.

Sometimes they will find a way of being born which defies many things. They will come to a mother who will feel there is no way she wishes to have child or has been told that she cannot have a child. If a Child of Light feels that that mother can indeed provide what they need, then where there is a will there is a way, and this is typical of what takes place. It can also be of course with a father, a man who has been told that he will not father children and yet, miracle of miracles, the wife conceives and a child is born. Where many children within a womb might choose to leave that womb and return to the security of spirit, a Child of Light is tenacious. It holds on to life, come what may. It will be born, it will survive the traumas of the early hours, weeks and months and it grows and flourishes and achieves its purpose.

One more question and we will bow to the fact that time is against us.

Q: A very strong sense of purpose could be a burden to some children. What about when a child starts to defy or resist that calling?

A: Indeed, there are cases when this occurs. There is a reserve within, a reserve which allows the spiritual contact with others like itself, still within the spiritual world, able to supply – usually during the time of sleep, of rest – the encouragement and to remind that child of the purpose. So with that taking place on a spiritual level, with the chosen guardian or guardians understanding and gently providing the environment where the child can thrive, with the right discipline – and this is important – the right discipline and the right freedoms so that the disciplines imposed are recognized as being necessary at that stage of growth, then the child comes through this torturous, usually adolescent, period. Because they are still human beings, they are still ruled by their emotions. It is just that they have a greater strength and ability to overcome than many other children will have.

We have truly enjoyed the inter-relationship of questions that have come forth today. The next time that we speak with you we very possibly will have a properly organized talk, followed by questions. But you never know with us, beloveds. We are indeed a law unto ourselves!

Our love surround you. May those who are having problems be showered with the light and love of spirit. Shalom.

All: Shalom.

Chapter 5

Talk Three, January

Abraham: Beloveds, Shalom.

All: Greetings, Father Abraham.

Abraham: We are very understanding of how it is when a new place is being used for the first time, how different the energies can be. But the way that each of you arranged within yourselves to follow first the meditation and then the rhythm of the AUM truly allowed the energies to grow in the way that we have come to expect. We always look for the different colours, sounds and such beautiful emanations to come from each to enfold all within their vision and this does, of course, enable such as myself to come and speak with you. Co-ordination of energy is not always understood to be as vital as it truly is. The medium or channeller, whoever he or she may be, cannot always adapt or adjust to the correct rhythm especially when a venue has been used for other matters. So this is an occasion when each one of you can offer towards ourselves that balance of love which we have come to expect when addressing such groups as this one.

Imagine for a moment all the life forces of soul that surround you within this place, all of those who have come on this occasion to imbibe, to share, to give of their own knowledge within the group so that from this we are able to determine what subjects are best to be spoken upon, what knowledge in a specific subject is required. Among these souls are those Children of Light yet to be born.

Progress within the womb

It is important to recognize that even after conception the spirit of the child-to-be does not remain permanently within the embryo but visits from time to time to ensure that the growth – mental, physical and spiritual – is as it should be. This is particularly important with those who have been entrusted with the future two or three decades upon the Earth. Their progress within the womb is a little different from those that are human but are coming to share what is taking place in the future but who do not have exactly the same trust as the Children of Light will be given.

Even when only a few months within the womb, the knowledge of the soul is implicit. Usually if there is to be a natural abortion this takes place before the third month. With the Children of Light this time span is a little different. Very often the mother may not be aware of her pregnancy until the second month is past. There are not the usual signs apparent. The pregnancy is calmer, more acceptable; there are less difficult problems noted by the mother-to-be; a sense of peace reigns throughout the body; a calmness of mind and of purpose relieves tension and disharmony which might reign within the home. So these are some of the first signs that the pregnancy may be different.

Children of Light are virtually always full-term babies. Now there may very well be those among you who will say, 'But we know of a Child of Light who was premature.' We would dispute how much of a Child of Light this infant may be. Be it the true Children, the Leaders, who will have a particular discipline to follow, a particular need to lead within the Earth or one of those children who will help the Leaders, help in very practical and often intimate ways to enable the changes to evolve. These infants [*the helpers or Followers*] follow a more usual pattern within the pregnancy.

Discipline and humanity
The Leaders of the Children of Light, their discipline begins from the very beginning and they follow that pattern throughout their full life span. This does not make them inhuman; it adds to their humanity because the example that they see surrounding them from their siblings, from their friends as they grow older, from the family in which they are born, can very often give conflicting signals to them. Not all are born to those parents who have knowledge, either of Children of Light or of the special need within the Millennium and the new age. Many are, but there are those that do not recognize these differences.

Part of your task, beloveds, as well as others with whom you may discuss these matters or who may read of our words, is to spread this enlightenment to those who you feel will be in need of it. We know that we ask occasionally that certain teachings be played down or not spread too rapidly, but in this case with so much doubt, so much hesitation among mankind of the changes of this age, it is important to be knowledgeable, to be able to help those who are in doubt and to spread enlightenment among them. So it is particularly your task and the task of those who understand our words to speak with those who are expecting children and one of the important aspects of your work is to allow your ability to divine to be acceptable within yourself as well as to others. By being able to divine we do of course refer to divination. How you do this best is your own decision. It can be with a crystal, it can be with linking with your Higher Self, with those aspects particularly helping your tasks or just your own psychic and spiritual awareness. This should help you a great deal in divining which of your friends or those you work with could be pregnant with a Child of Light. So your awareness must start from now, if it has not already begun.

None of these tasks will be easy. There will of course be those who will dispute this. They may even laugh at you and say that you are ignorant of the truth of life. But still help them, endeavour to enlighten them. The truly difficult people, ask them to be aware of certain signs within themselves that they may not have had with their other children, if they already have a family.

The quickening
The time of the quickening is very important. Sometimes it passes unnoticed by the mother but when bearing a Child of Light, there is a definite awakening of energy within that they know is the spirit entering their child. Sometimes it is a spiritual awareness, a linking with the God source that is felt by the mother, a desire even to be alone, to meditate, to form a link with the child that before had not been present. This normally occurs in the sixteenth week of pregnancy, and there may from time to time be little rhythms of energy that vibrate deep within, around the solar plexus, like communication taking place between child and mother. Where there is great closeness between the parents this may also be felt by the father and on occasion by older siblings. This can pass almost unnoticed if it is not shared with those doubters among us.

The birth is usually one that is more pleasurable. Very often the mother will request a particular form of childbirth that is more in accordance with her own awareness of her child's needs. Water births are becoming quite common for mothers of these children, feeling that the closeness and the gentleness of such a birth is more applicable to their child than in the past. Otherwise gentle music, gentle quiet people within the room, no bustle and haste or too much medical attention. It is of the greatest importance that the birth is natural and that the mother can hold the child to her very soon after the birth. This contact, bearing in mind that the child has not for a vast era of time come to the Earth, helps it to be aware of human contact.

Discipline of the soul

Seldom is a Child of Light the result of a Caesarean birth nor yet implements of any kind. The discipline within the soul has prepared the child for the birth which is usually quite comfortable. These things may not affect you personally but as you become more aware of your need to help others and share your knowledge with them, you will find these little suggestions invaluable. If you are able to help your sisters, your friends and your children understand more about these children it will help them as the children grow and to understand more about their strange little ways.

We have spoken before, and on other occasions outside of these particular talks, about how these children have a will of their own and we realize that some feel helpless in guiding them because they are so wilful. We can almost hear you saying, 'Discipline? Not within my child, there is no discipline and he or she will not accept it. What can I do?' Set an example within yourselves as parents. You as a child felt upset, angry, confused if your parents argued, if there was lack of consideration between your parents or for the children in their care. So think back into your childhood as to what was pleasurable for you. What did you most enjoy at an age when you can remember? What caused fear, that maybe there would be partings, desertion? Matters within the home that you could not comprehend. Try and eradicate this from your home, from your child's environment and encourage those with Children of Light to be equally aware.

Assertion

There is no outstanding indication, outside of the initial contact with the child after birth – we will briefly reiterate this: the immediate focusing of the eyes, the eye contact, the hello-I-know-you kind of look within them, the immediate understanding of intelligence. This does wane as the child settles into the normal pattern of growth and reasserts itself as the child is able to communicate their inner feelings with the parent.

Right from the beginning the assertion of will takes place. Try and be as spiritual as your circumstances allow within their upbringing. Explain why certain activities should not be undertaken when young, such as being on their own, such as using certain implements that can cause danger, but try and speak with them as though they are truly intelligent young beings. Do not ignore their questions. They are quite capable of understanding adult language and if it is not given to them they grow resentful. They should understand from an early age that discipline is important in their behaviour and also amongst other children and within the family.

Do not expect them to do what you will not do yourselves. Just because you are senior, more mature, it does not obligate you to place one standard to them and another for yourselves. How can they understand that a good night's sleep is important for their body and for their mental growth if you repeatedly do not retire until the early hours and then sleep on to mid-day? We know this is an exaggeration but you can see the kind of influence that such behaviour would have. You should not imbibe of things that you do not wish your children to – the most obvious, of course, is smoking, alcohol and drugs, even if they are quite mild. If you have to take a medication, explain to your child from at least the age of four, what it is, what it is for and why the child should not touch it. You will be asked questions, they will not refute what you are telling them but whether you can answer all of these questions is another matter. But do endeavour to be the example that you would like to have had for yourself as you grew.

Spiritual atmosphere
We have also spoken of the importance of a spiritual atmosphere but not necessarily religious, because these children, especially as they go into the world with their own purpose, will refute religion entirely. Now you might ask, 'But one of our Spiritual Teachers is Yeshua. What of Christianity?' We will remind you, Yeshua did not instigate Christianity. Yeshua instigated The Way, and The Way was a spiritual path to follow which included discipline, love, sympathy, compassion, knowledge and self-obligation to keep the body pure, as healthy as possible, and to be an example to others in all matters.

Even He failed on occasions, because of His human side. When He decided not to listen to the God force within Him, His Higher Self, then He gave way to human impulse and this would lead to anger, frustration, pain. When He did not recognize that certain things were given to Him to experience, to understand what others were going through but to overcome and in that way to find true growth, then He suffered. He suffered initially upon the cross because of His fear of undergoing what He had not experienced before – the very human side of any person when first experiencing pain – but He soon overcame this. He knew how to rise above physical pain and how to accept the humiliation of the punishment and turn it into an example of how to portray Himself before others. In other words, He turned the humiliation of the crucifixion into an example for others as to how to look toward light, beauty and peace within. He was, of course, the ultimate Child of Light.

Christ consciousness

As these children grow they will look toward the Christ consciousness as part of their discipline. They may decide that other teachers do not warrant their interest and that other religions, part of the Christian force, are too committing for them, too narrow because they have an instinctive awareness of truth. But they will understand the teaching that we give on the Christ consciousness. They will understand their own ability to link with God and with Yeshua for their guidance. This is important, to listen to these children or young people. Their ideas of what they feel they know and experience are very young. They may well be confused – the signals are confusing as with any newness, any change, and they are souls in very human bodies. If there is too much conflict within the home or the teaching areas of their scholastic approach then they will show that conflict and be very human in their response.

At this point does anyone present have a question which perhaps they have prepared from the other sessions that we have held with you that we can throw light upon?

Q: You have said that the children of fourteen or fifteen years old may be rebellious. Will these ones be the principal ones to have this revolt because they are the first, they have to prepare the way for the others to come through later?

A: Not exactly. There are of course now older children, as this has been taking place for nearly seventeen years so there will be a sort of revolt within industry now as well as in schools. You will find that these older young people will want to bring their ideas into the management or into their college life, addressing these matters to their professors, their teachers and to the management. Most of these, of course, have their own set principles and are not easily swayed or changed in the ideas that they have followed all of their professional life. So they will need such as yourselves and their parents to understand their need to bring change, to help them to bring a modification of change, not to rush into everything as soon as they become responsible within their own lives. They must learn to listen; not everything is bad that has been created before them but certain things especially within the schools must change and those who become teachers and ultimately professors, heads of schools, they will bring about radical change.

Now, you are asking, if this is so what of the normal children who do not come into this light stream? They will, as they have for centuries past, adapt. It is to their advantage that they adapt. They will recognize the strength, the leadership. And therefore in that way the other children will find a different acceptance of the teaching that is given to them.

These older young people must be made to see that so much of the traditional schooling is still important for them so that they are able to run the country, to be responsible for spiritual teaching, to be those that will guide the young, run the hospitals, change the medical system. It is vast and it will take two or three generations of these children to bring about these changes.

Another question, if you please.

Q: *I know two sets of parents who are both having difficulties in their own relationships and who both have Children of Light. Should these parents be encouraged to overcome their differences to the benefit of the children, even beyond their normal duty?*

A: Most definitely, and you as one of those who are a teacher in your own particular confines and beyond, have the responsibility to share this truth with those parents and lead them to a greater understanding of their own responsibility. Warn them as to what will take place if they ignore your help and direction.

Obviously they respect you, otherwise they would not share with you their fears and ask your help. Do not – how should we put this? – shy away from your responsibility. Tell them very firmly what they should do, using of course our teaching as your guideline. Do you think you would be able to have an influence on them?

Q: Yes, of course, but as a counsellor one tries not to influence but for them to find their own path forward and that's why I'm in this dilemma. Do I actually influence them to stay together for the benefit of the children and how severely do I do this?

A: If it is a case of parents wishing to separate, it should be more delicately handled. Because many Children of Light will be born to single parents or to parents who will in the future separate and who will have charge – perhaps only one will have charge – of the general upbringing and guidance of the child or children. So to try and influence them to stay together for the sake of the children can be a tenuous programme.

Your powers as a counsellor will need of course to change in many ways. A different form of counselling is needed for them to understand the nature of the children and what is required, but your usual form of counselling is still required to help them to understand their conflict and their feelings. So you would need to explain your feelings regarding their child or children, what will be necessary for the children to learn as they grow older and place the responsibility back to them to ensure this takes place. If they can do it better by moving away from a violent partner, or from a partner who cannot accept that responsibility, then they must make that choice, not you. And to evoke a response of remaining with a partner in deep unhappiness would influence the children incorrectly. So do follow your own guidelines, but with the additional explanations about how the children will affect the world as they grow to adulthood and as things very necessarily change.

Q: You have spoken in terms of the Western world, the teachings of Yeshua and the teachings of The Way. Presumably we are moving towards the teachings of The Way being spread throughout the world but there has never been one spiritual path the whole world is treading, there are Eastern and Western religions. May I ask what impact the Children of Light will have in the East?

A: They will, of course, initially be drawn into that line of spiritual contact which is their parents' and they will need to rely very heavily upon their inner guidance and the Higher Self source of guidance as well as those who will gradually infiltrate through the teaching in all parts of the world to bring a greater acceptance and acknowledgement of the path they tread.

The West has a great responsibility but it always has. When Christianity was first evolved and began to spread through missionaries to the more ignorant areas of the world, the pagan areas, they had the same difficulties in overcoming ignorance and paganism, but all paganism is not wrong. It is the attitude of those who say they have no strict belief but who do believe in the unity of the Earth and of man's ability to be part of the Earth that shows in its purest form: nature and love. So this also has a very deep place within the leadership.

Not all will, initially at least, look toward the traditional God for their guidance. Depending on their upbringing, they may well look upon nature and the God of nature, as they would term it, to guide them and as long as they follow the inner self and the love principle, they will be doing well.

They can share with those who have a stricter non-belief, the agnostics, atheists, to help them to understand that there is an influence within their lives that cannot be equated through science or mathematics. It can only be equated through the inner self and its gentle guidance forward within life, through emotions, through the ability of the human side within people to relate to others.

We do not usually find those who cannot accept a God force being cruel to others. In fact it is the very opposite; they have more respect, more understanding of the needs of individuals and they follow their own principles to the exclusion of those who have a fixed principle of religion and fight for it, kill for it.

What God, at any time through creation, has demanded the taking of life for the understanding of his existence? It is the misinterpretation of man and his desire to rule that has led to these infinite cruelties. These have reached a peak. We do intend, the next time we speak with you all, to speak of some of this, these iniquities, these appalling atrocities, and how, in your own way, you can influence them. It is very important that this responsibility in this area is understood.

The spiritual and the religious

None of this, returning to the fullness of your question, can come about in a short while. It is a long-term principle of teaching and influence. As those who follow the strict Muslim law, for example, or the strict Jewish law and any of the other 'followings' that take place, must be very gradually influenced so that they realize it makes good sense to release energy within the self to the acceptance of the spiritual versus the strict religions and the way that they have grown.

We feel that in the future there will be one more Pope. After this, the Popedom will cease. How it will come about, we cannot truly say but we only see outlined in the future the one leader of the Catholic Church emerging after the present one is deceased. Already man has seen the merging together of some of the religions, Christian religions, that have emerged from changes in faith, so that the churches are combined within their philosophy and in the truth that they share. There are even those, quite high up in the Church's principle, who now say they do not believe in the Second Coming nor yet in the immaculate birth or even in the principle of the Christian God. These are all indications that the changes are taking place. Therefore it is important to go slowly forward. Certain things that we are initiating now are the beginning of changes of principle so, of course we do expect you to incorporate them in your daily life. But others are more long-term, gradual, like the Earth diminishing within its size because of the swell of the oceans. These things take their natural course, the course of nature, but changes of impact, of principle must begin somewhere and they begin here, now.

My children, it truly has delighted us for your attention, absorption and the way that you are still approaching us for your greater understanding of our truth. We will look forward – and when I say we, it is all those spiritually present – to being with you again in a few weeks' time, with another subject and to ask more questions of you. May the blessing of the power of good enter this place, leaving its influence and its light for all who enter here to absorb and delight in, and our love, our blessing to all present, remain within your hearts and your minds. Shalom.

All: Shalom, Father Abraham.

Chapter 6

Talk Four, February

Abraham: My children, welcome. Shalom.

All: Shalom, Father Abraham:

Abraham: We have had our instructions: to be very careful with the vocal chords of our channel, [*on this day she was suffering from a bad cold*]; not to tire her by standing too long; and to be aware also of the need of those who are present to be able to ask their questions in order that sufficient information may be given to the group on the matter of the Children of Light. So we will endeavour, all of us present and myself firstly, to comply with all of these requests.

A greater audience

Interestingly, those Children of Light who have not yet been introduced into the world at this time, are extremely interested in these talks themselves – on a soul level, you understand. There are many thousands present in their soul form at this particular time. Now, it may interest you how to be aware of a soul presence, especially on such an occasion when your chakras are open, your minds are alert and when in general the spiritual aspects are around you and enabling you to understand what occurs in the spheres of light. You can, through your natural eyes, perceive them, in exactly the same way as you would perceive them if you were indeed in those spheres of light, as little dancing objects of light which appear in the air before you. Many people see these things but attach no importance to them unless there happens to be an occasion when they think, 'That is strange, those little sparks of light are in many colours.' They are not just white or silver but so often all the colours within the spectrum are indeed represented. So if you look at the air in front of you and become aware of these little dancing lights, you are seeing souls, and on this occasion you are seeing souls of Children of Light preparing themselves with knowledge before they are born.

The needs of the Children of Light

The last time that we spoke, we spoke of the nature of those children, during birth, during the time of gestation and also in very early babyhood. This time it is a little more of their growing into understanding and the way that they need to be helped. Do not just assume that because deep inside themselves they know their purpose, that this is on a logical level also. They are just the same as other children in wanting to enjoy themselves, to impress other people with their knowledge or their personality, but what does set them apart is their seeming inability to accept discipline. We know this has been mentioned before and it will be again, over and over.

Usually indiscipline in young children is tolerated very badly. Adults are aware of the importance of leading their children along the right path so that when they are adults they fit into society. At this point we say, what is society? What has created it? How did it come about that certain needs are presented, certain standards are required? If there are those that do not meet with this, why are they so ostracized? Why are they considered to be eccentric or working against the society of which they are a part?

We are painfully aware that many children of today are moving in such a pattern that they are difficult to teach. Parents are handing them over to the authorities. 'We cannot cope,' they say – but neither can the authorities. They have a very rigid, very strict understanding of how a child should behave. If they are different from this, then they pour them into a mould, thus creating endless difficulties for the years ahead. It is only comparatively recently that different problems within children have been recognized at all, that methods of teaching have changed in order to allow these children to aspire to far greater heights than they could have done even twenty or thirty years ago, let alone forty or fifty.

Dyslexia and disabilities
Dyslexia is of course the most common of these problems, but there are others also. There are those who are functionally deaf or blind; rarer of course are those that do not have the ability to speak. But the special schools for these children are very few, and qualified teachers for them are fewer still. We are encouraging those that come and speak with Master Joseph to take up roles in their profession which are a little different from the mass. Those who teach we ask to consider specializing so that they can be of greater help to what many consider to be backward children or children with learning difficulties, which are,

of course, the current words that are used. But so often when they are given the attention these children are found to be of a far greater intellectual level than the so-called normal child of the past and present.

Many of these children are Children of Light, and there is of course more than one type of child who is a Child of Light. Not all of them will stand out and be so creative, so full of energy and purpose that people will say, 'Behold! A Child of Light!' Ninety-nine out of a hundred people have never heard the expression and would laugh if they were told its meaning. People in general are no different than they ever were and they will not change to a great extent except those that are now growing into adulthood and are actually having things in common with these children that they can relate to. In another decade, of course, these children will become parents themselves and there will be a completely different organizational pattern of education which indeed we will applaud.

Education

Now, how to be aware of a child that does not fit into the general pattern of educational standard and yet does not appear to come into the alignment that we have given you regarding the Children of Light? How do we recognize their talents and how do we know whether or not as they grow older they do have a special gift which will be either a challenge to these children or will complement them in their tasks? You don't really know at a young age. It is only as they develop and as they are allowed to express themselves that they will do so. Parents who are too strict and who do not allow their children the ability to share with them their thoughts, their ideas and even their anxieties, will indeed harm the development of the child, whether it comes into this pattern or not. Likewise those who have too loose a hold on the rein will also spoil their children's chances of an adult life of perception, of control and of being able to choose adequately for themselves their path in life.

Don't worry too much about the spiritual path. This is the one aspect that these children can find for themselves, and they will. What is important is the educational path, the path of understanding fellow man, of recognizing the importance of discipline as well as knowing that there is always someone who not only knows better but will insist on taking on that role of leader in the society and will press down hard on those children that are rebels. If you happen to have a child or know a child who is a bit of a rebel, try talking to them like human beings. Explain that you understand, that the conflict, the anxieties, when you were young, although of a different time, are so very similar, that you will cooperate with them in ensuring that they are heard. And do encourage them to share their spiritual ideas.

The importance of dreams
One of the things that all these children have in common is their ability to translate the dreams they have and also to be so very aware of those dreams. To make a habit of discussing your children's dreams with them is a good one to get into. As they get old enough to read and write, encourage them to keep a little book to write down their dreams, especially the interpretation that might be placed on them. Hasten to calm any fears because some dreams that agitate are not always harmful. They could be there as encouragement or as a warning. So it is as well to monitor these dreams, these meditations that often your children will enter into, and in all ways to encourage them to share with you as their parents all that they are able to do. Many of them in adolescence will draw away and this often brings a sense of fear to the parents. Their child closes in on themselves, they do not even always appear to share with a sibling or with a close friend. In fact we have heard that many children can be together all day in an amicable manner, perfectly happy, never uttering a word. This is because they do have an ability to relate without words.

Their minds do actually move and entwine together with what passes for words between them but are actually thoughts which to them are very real and they might not understand when you say you hear nothing, you are not aware of what is passing between them. They need to be encouraged to share verbally with you what their ideas and thoughts are. You may find of course that your child may say, 'Why can't you interpret what I'm thinking? My friends can.' And then explain in your own words that the older generations find this difficult, that it is something that younger people are finding the clue as to how to do this and you would love to learn. Always enter into their space of communication. Never dismiss it, never laugh at it. If you do, you've lost your child. Certain things of course must be complied with, certain disciplines of the home. Cleanliness is very important. You can probably remember your own early days when it seemed less important to be clean than it was to be popular. It was only when you were older that you realized you were not popular if you were not clean! So there is always this interim time of growing where the child needs to be guided and helped forward.

Leaders and Followers

Now these different streams of Children of Light have begun to worry us. Everybody wants to know if their child is a Leader amongst the youth or whether their child will trail behind and only offer humble help. It really is not like that. It is not even like that in your own lives. You have free will, you have the ability to discuss, to argue, to offer your help. It would indeed be a very surly manager who would take no initiative from his staff, never ask for an opinion, and very often those who do fall into that category do not last very long within the employment. There will be a much greater interplay of activity with all of these children so forget about streaming them. We understand that in schools this is dying out also. A child is taken for what she or he understands and can learn and this is how it should be. One may be brilliant at mathematics and hate geography. Why not? When you are adult, if you are one of these, people are not constantly saying, 'But you must know geography.' Accept what you are good at, and as long as the child is not actively influenced during the school days against certain activities, a certain learning pattern, then as long as enough general knowledge on all the important subjects are absorbed, let the children gravitate to what they enjoy most because this is what they will do in adulthood.

We have spoken in the past of those who totally enjoy the crystals. Now these are indeed the purest stream of the children because they do come down from the Atlantean age. But it is not only these that enjoy crystals. We would hazard a guess that all of you here appreciate a beautiful crystal, but you don't all have your roots in Atlantis, nor yet in Egypt. You might well have had a life at those times; they might not be your most important lives.

A simple life

People undervalue the innocent simple life, as an ordinary normal person going through their days, understanding fellow man, reaching out toward the God force and allowing their soul to expand and grow. They want to be something greater – a name in history: 'I am Caesar.' Is being Caesar so wonderful? If it were I, I would rather not be Caesar. So why not be one of the soldiers at that time, that would listen to the words of the Christ and would see hundreds of people's lives changed by the demeanour, the words, the truth that came through Him? Maybe even being present at the Crucifixion and seeing the sadness and the tears and allowing the emotion to escape within themselves. That would be my choice, not to be the person who condemned an innocent man to death. But it is always the great ones that stand out in history, that people say, 'I'm sure my soul must have been around then. I know so much about it.' But never as an innocent; always as someone whose name was in lights.

If you find that your children are a little like that, wanting to lead but not really sure in what manner they should lead, help to direct them. We are quite sure that, through that direction, they will expand and grow, and those things that interest them particularly will be those things that they can teach and show to others as they come along and follow in their footsteps, wanting to learn, wanting to help, wanting to be at one with the new age and the new world.

When we speak next time with the children that we anticipate being here, we will speak to them of purpose. We will speak with them of determination, what enlightenment truly is. We will help them in every way possible to accept their role, not to undermine it, not to be afraid of it, not to have too large a head over it, because it should be as natural as being born and growing up and achieving should be. Think about the words spoken this day, beloved ones. They are as deep as you are going to get regarding these children. They are very much to the point and should be shared with all those that you come into correspondence with, friendship with or counselling with. Nothing dramatic, just sheer common sense.

Now we will allow our child to re-seat herself – we promised this – and when we have done this we will welcome your questions.

Who would like to speak first?

Q: I would like to ask how many Children of Light are around. I have a son who is a Child of Light, he is four and a half and I live in Norwich. What is the likelihood of him meeting other Children of Light in that city or the area around and are they liable to be of his age, or older? Or be able to travel to meet him? Or indeed at his young age is it important that he meets other Children of Light?

A: Your question interests us, my son, but firstly you sound very convinced, very sure that your child is one of these children. What gives you that opinion?

Q: *At a previous session with Master Joseph, he told me that my son was a Child of Light. That is all I have to go on.*

A: Well that is an excellent reason for believing it! [*Laughter.*] So, assuming that he is, firstly there should be many children growing around him within that area, within any area within Britain or the continent or what we term the civilized countries of the world that have more than their share of intellect amongst the people who live in those countries. So as he grows a little older and mingles with children either in his nursery or his school, you will find he will gravitate more towards those like himself than he will towards children who do not seem to have any particular gifts other than simply being a young child.

We feel you do not need to worry too greatly about these things but if in a few years the qualities that you feel from our teachings are not apparent, then have discussions with him as to any thoughts he has, memories that he might have, of lives that are not the now life. Sometimes these children do not wish to discuss this with their parents. They are afraid of being laughed at or scoffed at and yet most of them have an understanding of some life in history which is quite uncanny. As they get a little older and become interested in history, then of course this begins to come out within their conversation. There is one point here, however, which we know we've mentioned before, but it is worth reiterating and that is regarding the religions. Very few of them will be particularly interested in the recognized religions, but there could be a few who have an intense interest because their role is to broaden the spectrum of religious belief into spiritual understanding and teaching. They will be the true Christians who will recognize the Christ role, the role of leading the way so the religions will not totally die out. This would be a catastrophe. It could even lead to a return of paganism in its most difficult form, but they certainly will not

follow the old creed, that many these days feel is the true religion, but it is as you know man-made and will die a death.

Do you feel that we have answered your question suitably,
my son?

*Q: I would like to know whether I should encourage him to meet
other Children of Light.*

A: He will find them for himself. You may not know who they
are in any case, so might preclude a little friend who is indeed a
very spiritual and a very understanding person if you try and
monitor it. So we would not agree with that in any way at all.

*Q: Could you say if there is a certain way or method that the
Children of Light will show their spirituality?*

A: Gentleness, consideration for others, a love of those that are
afflicted in one way or another, appreciation of animals. There
will be many who will wish to be veterinary surgeons and, of
course, they will use the method of natural healing far more
than the traditional veterinary would do. Many of them will
become farmers and they will follow the present trend of
natural feeding, natural habitat for the animals and not necessarily breed animals solely for food. Some of them will appreciate bringing horses back onto the land to allow them to graze.
There will be many more animals that will graze together that
normally are considered to be enemies of one another, and
there will be those looking after animals in their compounds
that have a definite ability to speak with them and be understood, a rapport which many people have not yet regained. In
other words, the children of the present and the future will be
very similar to the people of ancient times, of many many hundreds and thousands of years ago when all of this was as natural
as breathing. So as well as understanding how important it is to
create a natural habitat for humankind, for their vegetation and
for their animal world, they will do it through love, not through
command or through fighting.

*Q: Father, your words just put me in mind of something in the
Bible, where somebody said: 'The lion and the lamb shall lie down
together and a little child shall lead them.' I just wondered if that
was perhaps a prophecy towards these times?*

A: Indeed so. There is a great deal within the Holy Book that is prophecy for this age which is only just dawning. It has a long way to go and a lot to be achieved within those years. But the more you read the Testaments, be it the Old or the New, the more you will recognize what is taking place now. You will recognize also that the teaching of your Spiritual Teachers is based very much on those ancient teachings recorded therein, because they are the true teachings and you can never walk away from the truth; you can only refuse to hear it.

Q: Father, my wife and I teach in what would be considered to be a leading girls' school, and yet even among these children there are probably ten percent who are dyslexic or dysfunctional. The way that it is treated seems to me to be purely physical and I sense that the dyslexia is more than that. Could you throw some light on the causes of the dyslexia and also how with some knowledge we could deal with these children?

A: It is basically a dysfunction of the brain which in many cases could even be overlooked because if the mind and the brain are moving together and coordinating with energy there is very little that cannot be overcome and a quality of life obtained to the ability of that child. For example, dyslexia has always been among us but was not truly understood until a matter of maybe forty years ago, if then, maybe even in more modern times than that. It often went with a kind of dullness of spirit, an inability for interest in anything profound – the village idiot of the ancient times was often a very severely dyslexic or autistic child who was not understood and whose salient points, excellent points within them, were never expanded upon or understood. As more modern times have come about with an enlightened approach to education and to children's needs it has been found that with certain approaches these children can make excellent quality of their lives and often will help other similar children to overcome and to exceed all possibilities within their own educational programme and what they wish to do. Mainly that is because the spiritual intellect of the mind is encouraging the brain energies to become more empowered so very largely the dyslexia is overcome through the endeavour of the child wishing to overcome it, understanding how much is being lost through the inability to write or to read in whatever measure that child has been prevented from learning.

In general they choose specific outlets in adulthood, outlets which are not specifically intellectual – or academic is a special word – you do not see them as a college professor or a mathematician, to name but two things. They do things that involve activity, which involve bringing people together with a like mind and a like need. They are excellent in this particular role. But as time passes medicine will understand more greatly which parts of the brain are most affected through the energy fields, the lack of brain cells, all these different things which are important. And they will be able to help with such factions as massage, especially that of the head [*coughs*]... forgive us, my son. [*More coughing. Water is offered and when the coughing continues, a prepared dose of cough medicine is suggested.*] It might be a better idea than the water. Do you think we will like it, my son? [*Laughter. Reply: 'It would be interesting to know.'*] A little sweet, to our taste. [*More laughter.*]

Now, how far did we get? With medicine. Now the different forms of massage or therapy which are now being encouraged by those of us who speak with you, such as the Craniosacral therapy, help to coordinate all the energies within the body and have a very vital part to play in helping the parts of the brain which produce dyslexia into overcoming it. There are other activities as well but this is the main one. This includes also hyperactive children and children who are apparently uncontrollable such as in autism.

Q: May I just ask a small supplementary question? You speak of the energies between the mind and the brain, does this mean that many children who are born with this dyslexia are not aligned, are not unified in themselves?

A: Indeed that is so, and many of the children who have the quality of the Children of Light come into this category because of their extremely high spiritual understanding and mind power which does not always keep up with the slightly slower brain which is of course usually defined by the DNA structure that it inherits.

Q: Do the Children of Light have the same life expectancy as ourselves? Do they have the ability to use crystals to lengthen their time on earth, to regenerate their bodies as in the time of Atlantis?

A: The second part of the question is a definite yes, but the first part is that they will not necessarily have a longer span of life because we cannot be sure in what area of the world they are born as to what kind of catastrophe could occur there which would shorten their lives anyway. In general however the children try to be born in an area where their life would have some expectancy of being able to fulfil itself in the role that they have undertaken. Do remember that it was hundreds and thousands of years ago that these children first dedicated their future to this time. So they knew the hazards, they knew the difficulties that would come about within the Earth itself, they knew how much man would welcome them or distrust them or seek them out to rid the world of them. They knew all these particulars, but they are still coming and they are coming in their hundreds and thousands. When this difficult stage of the world is past they will continue to come and will show themselves in their true light as the world becomes stabilized, far more pure, and really fulfil what God has desired for it.

Q: From what you've said about organic food and living off the land there seems to be a lovely pastoral, simplistic golden age that we are heading for. What part will computers and information technology play in the future? Are the Children of Light to be encouraged to use the new forms of learning?

A: Indeed so, it is all part of progression, it is all part of what mankind has been striving toward for many years. Remember that everything that appears upon the Earth in whatever form was already created within the spirit spheres, perfected there and then the idea implanted in the minds of those, scientific or medical or whatever they might be, in order to produce these things which will help man forward. Nothing can appear upon the Earth until the blueprint has been produced in those spirit spheres. The fact that the world is almost inundated at the moment with this particular form of influence is again non-coincidental. It is because these children are now growing into the state of consciousness were they will be using them – to great effect, we might say. Even the very young have a much quicker grasp of the computer jargon and abilities than some of their older friends and relations. So our answer is a most definite yes, but as always these things will reach a particular height and then they will fall back as other things come into being, and all those other things in the future will be more natural.

We recall a teaching which was given quite recently, a teaching regarding the spiral, how each spiral as it commences, commences reasonably slowly with things quite simple, quite basic and then as it moves toward the tip, it becomes faster and faster, with greater and greater knowledge, ability and growth taking place. This is usually the way that an age progresses. So of course at the end of the Piscean age, all the potential that was released into the world was indeed ascertained, understood and allowed to go forward, but the Aquarian age has begun more slowly. Have you already noticed, for example, how the days seem to be less short than they had been for maybe a year or two? A little more breathing space, a little more conscious thought and ability is beginning to take place. People can breathe again, metaphorically speaking. So this will continue; it will be almost as though the spiral is returning again to its beginning, but with all the knowledge that has been given in the past assimilated into the growth of man in order to allow man to expand and grow, taking back in that knowledge but adding to it so that as time passes, with that return to the simpler life, to the less hectic and crazy life, there will also be the ability of man to use his spiritual and mental growth in a way never known before. Dwell on this, give it really good thought and at some other time one of your Teachers will expand further upon it, if you desire this.

Q: It seems that we are making way for the Children of Light and in some future time there may be more Children of Light appearing on this Earth. May I ask, where are the other souls to go? Are we going to have learning experiences in other spheres of existence, in other realms? What is the destiny, so to speak, for the other souls that aren't involved in the future of the Children of Light?

A: Mostly those souls that do not return in the normal way of incarnation and reincarnation will return to the Higher Self and having shared all the knowledge that is within the Higher Self, they will go forward through other spheres, gaining knowledge in other dimensions on quite different progressive subjects than can possibly be learnt upon the Earth. So of course eventually it will only be the Children of Light upon the surface of the Earth and it will remain so until the world itself is no longer required within the galaxy. [*See also page 78.*]

We have really enjoyed this session with you all, and look forward keenly to speaking with the Children. We do hope that there will be five or six of them that can be present so that we can really speak with them and gain their understanding.

Until then, our farewells to you. Shalom.

All: Shalom, Father Abraham.

Chapter 7

Talk Five, March

On this day, the last of the five talks, five Children of Light were invited to join the group and listen to Father Abraham speak. They were all children or grandchildren of the group members and were aged between seven and fourteen.

Abraham: My children, welcome. Shalom.

All: Shalom, Father Abraham.

Abraham: It is a particular treat for us this day to be able to see the beautiful auras of the children as they are seated before us. We welcome you particularly, my children, to be able to speak with you, to explain a little more about the role of the Children of Light in the world today. Later on, if you have a special crystal with you that you would like to be blessed by those in the spirit spheres, then we will do this for you also. It will give us a lot of pleasure to answer your questions after we have spoken for a little while on the subject you have come to hear. Now we do realize that for some of you it is a new experience to speak to someone who does not usually come as a human being but speaks instead through a medium, as we call her, in order to express the teachings and the love that we have for humanity.

The life of Abraham

At one time a very long time ago I myself, Abraham, lived upon the Earth. I had a large family and many other grandchildren and nephews and nieces. At that time we would not all live in different homes, in different areas. We lived instead in a group of houses, or huts as they were at that time, in a compound which would be like having a big garden with many little chalets in it. It was in a way more fun than living at a distance because the children played together and knew each other very well. The grown-ups could leave their children in the care of other relatives and they could go into the mountains to pray, or to catch what food they could to eat, come back and prepare it, and then everyone would sit around together with their food. If it was in the evening and dark, a fire would be lit. This was important because there were many animals in the places where we lived – big wild animals – and the fire, the light from it, would keep the animals away. So everybody felt safe. In some parts of the world today people live in these communes, as they were known, and they enjoy doing this more than having their separate homes.

The Children of Light are being born all over the world. All the different countries with their many languages, the many skin colours of the people that live there, they all have these Children of Light. Now why do we call them Children of Light, you might think? This is because they have a very special knowledge deep inside themselves. Not just what is learnt at school or in your churches or taught by your parents, but a knowledge that comes from within the heart and the soul. That knowledge is about life itself, how to live that life, how to grow, how to help others, how to help the animal world, how to help to prevent people from the bad deeds that so many do. As you all grow up and become the same age as your mothers and fathers and have children of your own, you will look back on occasions such as this and see what a very different world you will be looking at from your adult eyes. No wars, no antagonism from one person to another; this will begin to happen. The natural disasters that you hear about – the forest fires, the terrible earthquakes – all of these things will become that of the past because the way that people live in the world makes a great deal of difference to the way that the world behaves, the Earth behaves, as well as to each other.

A Child of Light is one not only with this deep inner knowledge but the kind of personality that wishes to help others. A person who feels love for many, especially for other children and for animals.

Have any of you got animals at home?

J: [*a boy aged ten*] Yes.

A: What animal do you have?

J: I have a cat.

A: Just one cat?

J: No, two.

A: And what colour are your cats?

J: One's grey and black, and one's black.

A: And do they get on well together?

J: Yes.

A: And that is how it should be, should it not? In the cat world if they are brought up together they don't mind if they are multi-coloured, orange or gray or black or brown. They are a cat. So why should people, as they come into the world, worry about whether they are tall or short, or have a brown skin or a yellow skin or a white skin, or what language they speak? They are all human beings. This is what the Children of Light realize within themselves; that harmony, unity will be very important.

One thing that will please you a great deal, we feel, is that the type of schools will be different. You won't all sit in rows at desks having to learn certain lessons that people in government feel are good for you because many of you as you grow up will be the people in government. So you will be able to decide what is important for children to learn. Some children are very good at reading and writing and doing their sums, but others might prefer to play a musical instrument or draw or do some decorative work. Those children will be given the opportunity to follow what in their hearts they know they wish to do.

But this is quite a long way off. When your parents were small, things were very different from how they are in the world now, and your grandparents – some of them didn't even know what electric light was or have a cooker that was lit by gas, and that wasn't so very long ago. So those of you who think that 'Things will have to change a lot when I'm grown up', they will indeed have changed because life changes a great deal and very quickly. You might feel that this is a great responsibility, but you don't need to worry; it will be very natural. You will gently, calmly move into that kind of life, that new world without any problems. So do not worry about the future. Do what you are asked to do now, knowing that as grown-up people you will have the chance to alter things, to make things as you feel within your hearts that you want them to be.

Do any of you have any questions that you want to ask me, either about the Children or about yourselves?

THE CHILDREN OF LIGHT

J: I do, Father Abraham.

A: Then we are listening.

J: I would like to know, I met this boy and he had a nice energy and nice eyes and I wondered if he was a Child of Light.

A: One way to recognize another Child of Light is the way that they greet you and look at you when you first meet them, and how you feel within yourself. If you see someone and you feel, 'I would like that person to be my friend,' and they come forward and feel the same: it's as if there is some kind of understanding that is taking place, even without words, almost knowing how to think together instead of speaking together, knowing what each person is planning to do, that kind of companionship, then he is almost certain to be one of these children. As you grow up you might well find that your friendship lingers and as adult people you are still quite close.

But don't ignore other children who are a bit rough, those who don't understand your deep love for animals, for nature, for beautiful things, because they have their place in the world as well. As souls they have chosen to come into life and live with their Mummies and Daddies in the same way as you are. Because you did choose. In that world of light which is beyond the Earth where you now live, you had a choice. You were able to choose to come and to live with the people you knew would care for you and love you. So it is important always to remember this, that you have a choice and that choice will let you go forward in your chosen way, the way that you will be most content and find your greatest happiness.

Does anyone else have a question?

S: [*a boy aged ten*] I would like to know, which country should I live in, India or England, Father Abraham?

A: That is quite a big question, isn't it? India is a very big country. Do you have a particular part of India that you have in mind?

S: Well, it's in the north of India, a place called Dehra Dun.

A: And you are living there now?

S: Yes.

A: How do you feel about staying there for many years? Would you miss the country where you were born?

S: Yes.

A: So why make an absolute decision? Why not wait and see what the travelling is like when you are old enough to make your own choice, without having to ask anyone. You might find that there are no longer aeroplanes to take you from one continent to another. Now the reason for this is because the fuel that flies the aeroplanes comes from deep inside the earth. Some of it comes up through the big oceans and has to be refined before it is sold in the petrol stations and put in the cars and the aeroplanes, and that is beginning to get in rather short supply. So you might find that in another fifteen to twenty years, which is not so very far ahead, that it will be quite difficult to move from one part of the world to another. Then you will have to make a choice that is based more on where you are living when this happens.

There will still be boats, of course, and people who invent things, and many Children of Light will do this, will invent the kind of transport that does not need petrol and diesel fuel, so that the travelling might be slower, it might take longer but it will still be possible. Then you can spend some time in India, perhaps travelling around different parts of India to see how different people live, and some time in England, maybe also going to France and Germany and Switzerland and a lot of other countries. But it will be slower, it won't be so fast as it is now. We feel that will be good. You will have more time in different places to meet people, to see the changes that are going on. At the moment enjoy the country where you happen to be at any one time. Enjoy England while you are here and enjoy your home, your friendships, your country when you are in India. Does that answer you all right?

S: Yes, Father.

A: Has anyone else a question of this kind?

M: [*a boy aged fourteen*] You said at the very beginning that all the major natural disasters, like forest fires and earthquakes, would stop. How will this happen?

A: It will stop because of people's attitude to their world. At the moment there is a great deal of carelessness that takes place, because there are many who only care about themselves. They don't care about the people of other countries or people who have less than they have, or more than they have. Even in a country like England you see people go into the beautiful forests and they light a fire and when they have finished with the fire, instead of making absolutely sure that the flame is out, they leave the embers burning and there might be a little wind or something falls on the fire and it again shoots up with flames. Before you know what is happening, half the forest is ablaze, which is of course what is happening now in parts of the world. People's ideas, their consciousness as we call it, the thoughts they have regarding people and the world, the vegetation and the animal life, will become less harsh. There will be a greater understanding and sympathy, we would call it, so people will be very much more careful when it comes to using too much of any fuel.

Thoughts as well, unfortunately, can cause earthquakes. When people are unhappy together, causing warfare, the angry thoughts affect the Earth. The Earth is living, it is not dead. It is as living as you are. It hurts when things are done to it that destroy it. It is like having a mind that thinks about how to prosper. The trees and shrubs do not just come into life and flower in the spring; they have a consciousness and they know that that is the time when the weather becomes warm and the rain falls, that it is time for them to blossom. So they have a very wonderful inner self and if mankind is destroying them they react. Many of the earthquakes take place in parts of the world that are destroying mankind through arguments and wars.

So as the Children of Light grow up and realize that war is bad it will cease. They will talk instead of fighting. So you see the Earth will react differently and there will be more calmness and peace in the Earth as well. There is something that you can all do to help the Earth: you can think about the power that is deep, deep, deep inside the Earth, think of all the natural resources that are beginning to fail and in your mind, think to yourself, 'They are replenishing, they are growing,' and your thoughts will make this happen. It is really very simple. If you want, say, one of your animals to love you, you stroke it, you talk to it, you love it. If you hit it, or ignored it and didn't speak, or shouted at it, it wouldn't love you and it would probably go away.

So the Earth is very much like this. So when you say your prayers, ask that the Earth be made whole, that the Earth lives, that it is vibrant with beauty and you will see around you that this will happen. A garden that is loved, that you plant flowers in and seeds that become trees, looks beautiful; but a garden that is just a patch of earth and nothing put on it to grow is virtually dead, it has no beauty, no harmony. So if you remember always to treat the Earth like you would yourselves and make a promise to yourself that as you grow older you will remember these things and continue to do them, that they are not just for when you were young but for when you are older as well. To teach your own children to love, to have compassion and not to dislike. Then that vibration will continue and you will live in a beautiful world with lovely plants and trees and forests and lakes and grasslands to walk through without the pollution and without your bodies failing you. You will be strong and healthy. With some of you, you might be quite elderly before these things happen, but with others it will start to happen after the year 2000, the new Millennium in two years' time, is part of the world, the universe.

We hope that at that time you will all come and speak with me again. Then you can tell me the changes that have taken place in your lives, in your schools – because if you don't tell your teachers what you would like to learn, how can they know? As you grow older they will listen to you, much more than they do now. And some of you may become teachers and you will listen and speak to other children who are small.

We could talk to you for a long while, but we know that your attention is good, therefore we will cease speaking and instead we will suggest that those crystals that we see in your hands which are really glowing, full of energy, full of life – can you feel that in your hands? Can you feel that your crystals are almost warm in the palms of your hands? For we see that warmth, we see it as a beautiful glow as though it was a light. So if you would like us to give a special little blessing with your crystals, we suggest that you come one at a time and place it in my hands so that we can do this.

Thank you. What colour is your crystal?

C. [*a girl aged nine*] Green.

A: Do you know what the colour green does? (**C.:** No.) It is for harmony. If people are not very well, if you put a green crystal near to the part of their body which is hurting, the pain goes away. It is a crystal that we say is for balance, for healing. Does anyone else have a green crystal? We will give that one back to you. We have blessed it for you. And if someone else with a green crystal likes to come, we will tell you if it is different.

Thank you. Now this crystal we feel is very, very like the other one. Do you understand about vibrations? Do you know what the word means? Well, a vibration, for those that are not quite so sure, is a sound, it is a movement, an energy. And some crystals have this same energy and others are very different. But this one is very similar to the first one that we held, and this can also be used for healing, especially headaches.

Is there somebody with a different coloured crystal? And what colour is that one?

C. It's clear and it's got purple in it.

A: This one is also a healing crystal but it heals in a different way because it has a different vibration, a different energy. The energy of this crystal is much faster so if you can imagine that a green crystal moves t i c k t o c k, t i c k t o c k like a very slow clock, and this one is a little faster, tick tock, tick tock, so it has a very clear message for pain. If you know someone, or if you yourself have a pain in your tummy perhaps, a crystal like this helps to calm it, because it raises the vibration of what is causing that pain and makes it go away. You will have to think about that a little bit but we know you will understand.

Any more crystals? What about you, my son, that asked us about the calamities of the Earth? That is a wonderful large crystal, is it not? And what colour is this?

M. It's mostly clear with pink backing.

A: This one is not so good for healing. It has another purpose. We would use this crystal in order to raise the vibrations for meditation. Do you meditate at all?

M. I don't think so.

A: Meditation is going quietly within yourself and having thoughts about things that are spiritual, thinking about the earth, for example, nature, how animals are different from human beings, how all the different plants are so different, the different shapes and sizes and smells – that is meditating, it is deep thinking and it is usually done when you are on your own. Now a crystal like this, if you place that in front of you – the best way to meditate is to sit on the floor like some of these other young people are doing, and you place a candle and light it with your crystal next to it and you think quietly about how things can be changed to be beautiful. So we wouldn't use this one to heal anybody, but it would be excellent just for you, for yourself, to quieten your mind and to give you thoughts that will affect the Earth in the same way as prayer does.

Do you understand, my son? We would like at some time to speak with you on your own, if you would like that, because we can tell you a lot of things. All right?

Now, anyone else with a crystal?

A: This is a nice solid crystal as well. And what is this one called?

S: I think that's a quartz crystal.

A: And the colour, because there are different kinds of quartz crystals?

S: See-through with bits of white at the bottom.

A: So it's very clear like glass would be, is it?

S: Yes.

A: And do you use this for anything special? Because we feel that a crystal like this would have quite a lot of protection in the room where you are. It is largely a rough surface but it has a smooth surface going to a point, and crystals like this can give energy within a room, allowing that room to be a safe place to be in. Do you have it in the room where you sleep?

S: Yes, we do.

A: It is a good crystal for this. Do not have it too close to your bed. In fact no crystal should be too close because it can take energy away from you instead of giving it to you. [*The only crystal that should be kept in a sleeping room is clear quartz*] You were going to say something?

S: We have crystals on our wall, on a shelf.

A: Do you? And you have a light that shines on the crystals?

S: Sometimes we light a candle.

A: Do you notice your crystals change their colour when you light a candle near them? No. Well, you look out for that because the warmth and light, the natural light of a candle, changes the energy of a crystal. The energy in a crystal decides its colour, so a very clear but dark crystal becomes lighter if the energy becomes lower. So that is something for you to look at the next time you have a candle that is near to this crystal.

There should be one more crystal, am I right?

A: Thank you. Ah, now we have a wand. Do you use this wand for anything special?

H: [*a girl aged seven*] I use it for healing.

A: It feels very clear and yet within it there is movement, as we call it. There are lights beginning to grow inside the crystal which respond to energy, and the energy of giving healing to someone changes the quality of the crystal over many months, not in a very short time. Now the medium we are talking through has the crystal here which is very clear but at one end of it, it is beginning to change. There are little lights and feathery things beginning to grow in it because she uses that to remain calm and peaceful while we are speaking. So it is changing its energy and one day it will be so full of energy that she will not be able to hold it and she will have to have another new one. So you will find, if you use this a lot for healing, it will begin to change and that can be very exciting.

We have held all the crystals now, have we not? We hope that you enjoyed the little talk that we gave to you, and that when you feel like it, you can come and you can either talk with me, Father Abraham, or with Master Joseph and ask any questions that your parents cannot answer for you. They know a lot, but they don't know everything. [*Laughter.*] We don't know everything either, but we do know a lot. [*More laughter.*]

Do we have much more time, my son?

Chairman: About five minutes.

A: Well that once more has been quite clever, has it not? We are always given one hour in which we can speak and after that hour we have to go away again. So mostly we know this and sometimes those people that we come and speak with, they know it too so they make sure that all their questions are answered by us when we are in the same space with them.

One day we will talk to you about time, because it is a very interesting subject, but we will leave you with one thought: that in the sphere of light where the Masters live, there is no time, no clocks, no watches, but we never wonder what time of day or night it is, because there is no daytime, no night-time, there is just beautiful light that we can live with and in.

So now you have been so good and we are so proud of you. So we say goodbye until once more we can come and talk with all of you, like today. We thank all of you parents for having brought your children to enable me to speak in this way and give them a little knowledge as to what lies ahead.

So we say farewell to you all. Shabah Shalom.

All: Shalom.

Chapter 8

Questions and Answers on the Children of Light

This section is made up of individual paragraphs from trances over the last ten years. Some were given in response to questions and some were spoken by the Teachers themselves in the course of discourses on other subjects. They are gathered here in subject headings but are not necessarily sequential.

First Inklings

There is, within the outer planes of the universe, a place where the souls that dwell within it have no further need to return to the Earth. Their knowledge is complete – they move totally within the Law, and are soon to be absorbed into the great ether, that energy which began the Earth billions of years ago. They were approached and agreed to come again to be born in man and to try and bring their influence into the world – their greater understanding and moreover their love vibration. So many of these souls are descending to the Earth and being born again in the young children of Earth. So many of you are aware of these beautiful souls, their eyes look upon you with understanding and with knowledge. They are like no tiny child was before, and as they grow, the knowledge within them will be able to be used within your world, and the fruition of this new age will take place.

These children will grow, and they also will bear Children of Light, and as the generations pass, so will the evil. so will the darkness, for they will live happily together and they will create a positive force of energy where negative energy is now prevailing. By the end of the next century to this one, the pattern of the Earth will have changed. All those that do not look toward the light will have left the world, never to return upon it. The Children of Light and their children and those such as yourselves that seek to propagate truth, you will remain, and will prosper and learn.

Changing the world through thought

It has become imperative that those who are in tune with the light should use the light to overcome darkness and evil. You may think that those such as yourselves seated here and listening to us are the ideal people for such a task. It may surprise you to realize that there are those who are far more suitable, and they are very young indeed. The Children of Light, about whom we have spoken so many times, have themselves that direct line to spirit, a total awareness of what is needed within the Earth. Though many of them are very, very young, and cannot at this time portray their feelings in words, their soul is active on behalf of their bodies, and their soul is active on behalf of the world. It is our fear, my children, that they may lose this ability as they grow older, because of the attitude of their parents and teachers, and others who cannot recognise their potential and their ability. It is in this way that yourselves can help. You can be aware of their light through the way they speak and behave, through their refusal to conform to the life that everyone has found perfect to the present time; and notice particularly those children who have this ability. Extol them to further efforts. When they are adult, they will then show great phenomena. They will be able to change the world by thought. Until this time occurs, those of us who are able to influence the spiritual in man must endeavour to exhort him into what can be done, into speech and into action.

Where do the souls of the Children of Light come from?
This is now a generation where some of the souls that are incarnating now have not done so for millions of years. They last dwelt upon the Earth when the souls were still able to commune with the higher realms and when the mind of man was not so tethered by his ignorance. They have spent aeons of time within the spirit realms learning – attending the Halls of Music, sitting at the feet of the Masters in the Temples of Learning, and acquiring the art of meditation and tranquillity within. They have a very special light, a light obtained from knowledge, and their vibration is higher and faster than most of mankind.

They have come to live upon the Earth to help man to enter the new age, to be more aware of the potential of life as it should be lived. They dwell among you now and many appear to those who have lived for many years in the world as it has developed, to be at variance with law, to be rebellious. They desire not to live in the old pattern, to gain for the sake of riches and wealth; they prefer to live within themselves and among themselves, absorbing the light and continuing on their own pathway, oblivious of the needs of others – but they are not, my children, oblivious of the needs of others. They know well the density of man and how impossible it might be to raise the vibration of the world and save it from ultimate disaster. You will not make of these children the lawyers and the doctors, the business men and the merchants; you will find among them the Teachers and the Masters yet to come.

The Children of Light who are being born at the present time, carry within themselves the seeds of great illumination for the world. Those born within the Piscean age still need guidance. They will also need to guide and help the Children of Light as they mature, for the Children of Light are aware of the teachings, but they are not so aware of the laws of man. They desire to fulfil the universal laws, and to allow the laws of man to go unheeded. So those of the Piscean age must be aware of this and endeavour to help them. They cannot, however, help anyone if they are not aware of their own purpose in life.

Recognising the Children of Light

Many of the Children do indeed exhibit a rather old-fashioned, courtly behaviour. It is as if they are living in past times when the gentlemanly and lady-like behaviour was worth so much more than young people of today seem to warrant. So that is indeed a classic amongst these children. All of those who have come to us personally for our enablement to guide them – and they have ranged from between four years to about fifteen – they all had this quality. And we have also been aware through parents or grandparents describing them that they are indeed very wise children who do not behave as other children do but seem to have an awareness of what is right and wrong at a very young age.

Leaders and Followers

There are two kinds of Children of Light. There are those that will be the Leaders, and there are those that follow behind, equally aware of their purpose and of the love within them for the universe, prepared to do all that they can to help the Leaders to accomplish. But without yourselves as parents and grandparents, as godparents and friends, as those who teach within the schools, without such as yourselves, how can they accomplish? For they have hearts that beat within the human breast, and they can feel as discouraged as others who try so desperately to show love, and find that it is rejected. If each here speaks to another on words of trust and words of truth, the message quickly encircles the Earth. Gradually, as this century comes to its close, the evil manifested by the few will decline. Love, manifested by the many, will increase.

The earthly guardians of the Children of Light

For the last hundred or so years, there have been many movements endeavouring to link the spiritual planes with the earth-world, and great advancement has taken place. Circles such as yours have helped to link the spiritual and material together. Now these circles must be aware of the ultimate truth, must create within the energy and light which will go to the dark areas which will surround the Children of Light. Together there will then be illumination and help and the ultimate tragedy of the cessation of peace within the world will then be averted.

The life force within them is total – it is the harmonies of love – but they are yet infants. Until they are grown and have propagated the like unto themselves again and yet again, there can be no true change in the climate and vibration of your world. But your part is important – you will help them to grow and understand the earthly laws until they are of an age where they can change them. You can provide the environment and the light and love in which they may grow. You can stabilise the spiralling pattern surrounding your Earth by prayer, meditation, communication with your Higher Selves and thence on through the spheres, until the Creative Force itself assimilates and recharges the light to surround the earth.

We have spoken many times of the Aquarian age and its purpose, but in this particular respect, the souls like yourselves that have returned many times and are expanding spiritually within these lives, have a great responsibility to others, for their actions can either destroy the world or enable it to recover the equilibrium lost. It is not enough that the Children of Light that are being born have such knowledge, for they need direction, and those that are learning spiritually in their early or middle years, must direct these young ones and accept responsibility for their lives.

The role of parents

Where the Children of Light themselves are concerned, their own great inner knowledge of spirit will sustain them, whatever the outward distress may bring. They have the ability to read your mind, they will look deep within your eyes and see there the love and richness that you wish to surround them. Words will largely not be necessary between you.

It is the parent upon which to concentrate, to endeavour that their ignorance does not cause bodily harm to the child because of their inner fear of that child's ability and learning. Mankind has a great fear of that which he does not understand, and some of these children will be born to parents who do not have that understanding, who may misjudge the quality of their child; but again, that child will have chosen, and its path upon the Earth bears the same lessons as generations before. None can escape it, even those of such quality of understanding.

As it is with older people within this life who are upon the last step of life's journey, they too can experience fear, both of what lies before and what has lain behind; and so it is with these children. They have memory of what cannot be surpassed and that which mankind cannot remember consciously. If you have the opportunity to talk with them, allow them to express themselves with what their memories are; assure them of your love and your knowledge. No greater act of kindness can be served upon them. As time passes, you will know what to do without being guided, for the children, as they enter their roles as teachers, they will show you exactly what it is they need.

Watching over them

These Children have a task before them that as yet has not been revealed. They still are children, they still need love and understanding, they must still be taught as man has always been taught throughout his lives; but their will must not be destroyed, they must not be held back until all desire to lead is banished from them. There are those among you that have memories of childhood that are sad. Do not allow these children to have similar memories. Let their childhood be full of laughter and singing and happiness, for when they grow older, it will be full of the earnestness of leadership, of allowing their Earth to survive the horrors of war, the errors of natural disasters brought about by the ignorance of their forebears in their ancestry of Earth.

Natural disasters

They too have been born in the same way as any other child has been born, but there is a difference. Mankind from the moment of birth has no memory of the past, no memory of a spiritual existence and no memory of a past existence on the Earth, therefore that young new child begins life ignorant of life, and needs to progress in the same way as it has done for millions of years. But these children, they have memory, memory of the spiritual lives that they have enjoyed upon the Earth, and memory also of the spiritual life in the spheres of light. These children will grow as others. When they reach maturity they will be the leaders, the teachers; they will be those that will represent the leaders of the countries. Gradually they, and those that are born from them, will prevent the wars, the destruction that has begun to envelop the world. All that is occurring now is within the great plan of life.

The many millions of souls which now inhabit the Earth are due to return to spirit, to enhance themselves once more in their etheric soul bodies, and they will not return again to the Earth until it is stabilised, until once more it is a place of beauty and learning, inhabited instead mostly by these Children of Light. There will of course also be many others that are born, but the souls within them will be aware of their task to rehabilitate the Earth.

The many different countries within the continents upon the Earth will be more sparsely populated, and this is having its effect already – the internal wars within the countries, with so many returning to spirit. Other continents will find similar events occurring, the 'natural disasters', so-called, the earthquakes, the flooding, the erosion of land by the oceans, this is all part of the cycle of life for the completion of this present age – the Piscean age.

Restoring the world

We spoke with the souls of the Children of Light and they were eager and ready to send aspects into your world now, in order to create that purpose and that light. They must have a teacher, a leader. They must also have those that love them in the physical form upon the Earth, so the parents of these children are very carefully chosen by their souls. The parents truly have no choice, it was indeed the Children of Light who chose where to be born, when to be born, and to whom. They are confident that as they grow and learn from the experience of those that bear them, that they will follow the direction of the Lords of Light, and they will bring into the world the harmony and peace that it craves.

Your actions are very important, your prayers are crucial. To link with the light, to have a candle before you, to look deeply within it, to imagine that that candlelight is burning within the centre of your Earth, restoring energy, restoring everything that is needed for the Earth to survive. You would not realize, beloveds, how close your world has been to extinction. This is the third movement* within the spiral and it could well have been the last, but the Creative Principle, that which is God, has great faith in the men that have arisen from His thought, and therefore, the crucial time has passed and the Earth will arise again in all its magnificence and glory. The sad thing is, it may not happen within the lifetime of those present, but it will begin to be restored as the Children of Light reach maturity and give birth to their own offspring and bring them up in knowledge and truth.

The gift we can give them
Show them how to love. Those that have perfection and move to a constant vibration of pure spiritual love find it difficult to understand human love. They have not within them the same basic desire and need for reproduction, for learning how to show their love, how to create and how to be tender and kind. They must be taught these things, they must learn compassion, they must learn tolerance. When there is perfection, it is difficult to tolerate less. Show them love, teach them the laws of man, for they will have no conception of this. They will teach you the laws of God.

They have this total knowledge of universal law, of love, and it is to this that they will adhere and try to teach others. They are not easily guided to the ways of man and to the misconceptions that man has adhered to and brought historically into his present. Their very understanding of the purpose of life will evoke the change within mankind. Anything that is said or done to them will be of no avail. The change will be in yourselves and not in them. The beauty that shines through their eyes and through their understanding will increase with their age. They are pure light; the only anger that they express is that of the anger of ignorance and intolerance to which they may be

* In previous talks the Teachers have said that our current civilisation is actually the third to grow and flourish on Earth. The first was that of the Els and the second, the Atlanteans.

subjected. Allow them the freedom of expression that they need, but guide them well; allow them to see that the man-made laws must be adhered to until they are old enough to change them with their inner wisdom, and which they will do; but above all, show them that quality and quantity of love which they need, it is important to their mental and spiritual development.

On limitations

Be realistic, my children, recognise your limitations. Try not to appear before others in a mask you cannot keep. It is better to remove the mask, admit that there are other things you cannot achieve, although you desire to, and in so doing you will have a greater strength. Then perhaps these Children of Light will receive true teaching. They will know who they can rely upon to guide and help them. They also will be able, as the ancient Egyptians, to travel in the state of sleep, to see the dangers that are coming to the world, whether from armed beings or from danger through nature. Although the world is nearly in this twenty-first century, and the Aquarian age, the age of fulfilment is encircling it, very little can be done toward that fulfilment until man lays down his arms and looks up to the eternal light for his guidance and his majesty and beauty, until man realizes there is one influence only, that of the Cosmic Light.

Tolerance and patience

Your own part in this, my children, is clear. Some of these young ones are either your own issue or are related to you, your children or the children of your kin. It is your duty to be their spiritual sponsors. When they turn to you for guidance, that guidance must be pure, it must be as we have initiated within you. The truths must be allowed to issue forth upon your breath, that they may be confident and aware of their purpose. Not only within your homes, but elsewhere in the environment, these children will need guidance. They will not adjust easily to the shortcomings of man. So pure is their light and so clear their inner understanding, they will be impatient with mankind, and also will be impatient with slowness and weariness of change. But this next period of time is so important to those of you here, and those others that link with us to imbibe the light and feel its energy stimulating the chakras and working within the body.

A challenge

The present young, the Children of Light, have come a long journey. They have come from forces of great light. No longer did they need to live within this Earth, but they have given up the progress that they can only achieve in greater planets of light, and in giving up this progress have come to lead you and allow your fulfilment within this life. How many of you have the dedication to lead them through the maze of laws made by man? How many of you can lay aside your own vanity and listen when they speak? When you are very old and they still have youth, will you be led by them, see your laws destroyed and changed, give up much for which you have fought and laboured throughout your lives, so that the beginnings of the future may be laid?

Healing

Listen to these very young ones, the words of wisdom that fall from them. Look into their eyes. See the way that they heal; see the way that they heal not only fellow man, but also nature. They will have the ability to allow a spring to gush forth, without the way that man has done this for thousands of years, with a staff, but with their hands, bidding it to arise from the soil. Very soon the drought that is destroying many parts of the world will be no more. That which is deep, deep within the earth will be bidden to rise.

In this new age, as the Children of Light are born, they will recreate among themselves things of the ancient past, for they will believe and they will transmit light and energy particles and create healing on the metaphysical level. But these children are only now being born. It will be many years before their influence is felt. Those preceding them, who are now bearing these Children of Light, will have a spark of intelligence and understanding, and it is hoped that they will accept the mind power of their children for the Children of Light have within themselves that power of light to dispel the darkness. They will not abide by man-made laws, for they look only to the spiritual laws for their direction; but it is these children who will ultimately save the world from disaster.

The cycles of time

We have spoken much this day of light. Deep within our own hearts there is the knowledge, the awareness of the festival of light which has been encircling man for the last few days. We call this worship of light 'Chanukah'. It celebrates the arrival of the Children of Light, two thousand, four thousand, six thousand years ago, each one as they move away from an area of darkness and walk toward Utopia.

Six thousand years ago it was a tribe of the Indians that moved across the borders of the vast area where they lived, seeking new pasture, desiring within themselves to be able to be much stronger, much purer within their spirit. Four thousand years ago there were those that came out of a darkness, led by Moses. He brought them vision of a promised land; how sad that they did not realize that it dwelt within their hearts and constantly they looked from hilltop and mountain toward the terrain before them, desiring so much to be the first to see that land. Many died upon the way; it was sad, but in that act of dying they had found their promised land, and in their searching they had given much to others, even those that could not profit because they could not lose the old ways of thought.

Two thousand years ago another light was lit, another candle glowed in the darkness of the cave, and as a young child made His entry into a saddened, darkened world, that light became flesh. Now at this time, what of the world now? Does any light shine? We see many, but we see them coming from each dwelling, however poor, however great, we see that light moving up and out, and as droplets falling over all that stand in their way. This is the way of light as is the way of all Truth within existence. It must permeate, it must come deep into the souls and hearts of Man. It would not be true to itself if this was not so.

The future
Imagine these children full grown with all their knowledge drawn from the dark and the light, balancing it with their intuitive powers, conferring with the Higher Self and the cosmos also, begetting their own young and them also. Project your minds, my children, to one thousand years hence, and visualise the world as it is intended to be. The beauty, the clearness of the unsullied skies as fumes and illness depart, as man returns again to the land and ceases to struggle for richness and wealth, and seeks instead the harvest of spirit. See the great skies open and visualise the heralds of night as they come and mingle with Uranus's [*the planet of the future*] children.

Pollution

This decade of time, leading toward the year two thousand, is a time of preparation for those who are still within the world to achieve their ultimate soul purpose. At the end of this decade there will be many who will return to their spiritual spheres, their task done, and those that are among the Children of Light will have reached a certain maturity which will enable them to begin to work in a co-ordinated way with their peers, and influence them in the way in which they know inwardly and spiritually their life will unfold.

At the commencement of the new millennium there will then be an influx of new births. These will be the souls that desire greatly to be aware of newness, to be aware of the completion of the old as it takes its place in history and allowing that which no longer has any place within the reality of the world to be relegated to history itself, that future man may read and be aware, and learn from the mistakes that have been made. By this time also, a great deal of the pollution which is reaching its height will be diminished, as it becomes more and more apparent in different areas of the world that if strong action is not taken against the elements causing the pollution, mankind is liable to become extinct.

This will reach its ultimate force when the Children of Light mature sufficiently to take their rightful places as the Leaders, spiritually and in the world of commerce, bringing about their deep inner knowledge in a practical way. Meanwhile, in the remaining few years there will be great influence brought upon mankind to change the way of his life, to become more aware of his surroundings, of the countryside which is in his power to rescue from the degradation that is now taking place, to try and cure the deep pollution within the sea. This will help the cleansing process to continue through the natural disasters provoked by the need of the planet itself.

World leadership

The Children of Light are expanding in numbers upon the Earth. The country in which you dwell does not have a monopoly upon these children. They are born throughout the entire world, and once established in life, as they grow up and form a union, others also will be born, and these children will be those who will be the leaders, the teachers. They will be the Presidents, the Prime Ministers, the ruling families. In time to come, much of the evil that is present in the world at this time will have dissipated, because there will be a greater intelligence and a greater flow of light established within mankind. At that time, and not before, many things are waiting to be unlocked; they will indeed occur.

Crystals
We have entered into the Crystal age which is evolving with the Golden age and the Aquarian age in one vibration. The birth of the Children of Light has been synchronised so that they reach the age of wisdom as the memories and the energies within the crystals are becoming awakened to their true work.

The Christos
We wish to speak for a few minutes regarding the Christos. We are asked so often whether there is another being within the Earth at this time who carries that same light, who is perhaps another Christ to teach in this age. Our reply is that there will be such a one to be born – not to take the place of Jesus the Christ, who spoke for God two thousand years ago, but one who will show to the world again the Way, the Truth and the Light. This child will be born in the normal manner, will grow, will lead the Children of Light forward as an army of beauty. In many years to come, that child will be acknowledged as bearing the Christos within. All humanity have a thread of that Christos within them, because all humanity have a soul within, and that soul bears this light.

A great teacher
A great teacher will come again at the beginning of the Aquarian age, that the teaching will again, though simple, be very dramatic in the qualities that are presented. The Children of Light, as they grow and their awareness is shared one with another, will have leaders among them also, and when the teacher decides to be born in some part of the world that needs so desperately to have one with great understanding, who can lead man forward to a better life, then the Children of Light will recognise that leader, that teacher. It will be like a vast congregation of disciples, not just twelve, but a multitude, feeling the call deep within their soul bodies, united, happy in the understanding that at last change can be perpetuated after so many centuries of hardship and gloom.

The Higher Self, Soul and Reincarnation

Initially soul was one vast energy field. At a particular point in evolution this exploded into a myriad of particles which gathered together into Higher Selves. The Master has often said that it is difficult to explain the true nature of the Higher Self. Language itself is based on what individuals see around them, and it is difficult to understand what cannot be perceived.

Each individual soul is an aspect or particle of a Higher Self and each Higher Self contains more particles than there are cells in a human body. Not all aspects incarnate, just as a woman has the potential to conceive hundreds of children in a lifetime and may only actually give birth to two or three children. At the end of life the individualised soul returns to the Higher Self and the experience and learning of that life is shared throughout the entire Higher Self. Once an aspect has incarnated it cannot return; each aspect or cell of the Higher Self can only incarnate once. Because of this, when a soul returns, something akin to a conference takes place where the karma is reviewed, the experiences and understanding of life are evaluated and a new aspect steps forward, with the essence of the previous life within, to take the learning forward.

If the Higher Self could be seen, it would resemble a vast rainbow, and the particles that comprise it are organized according to the colours of that rainbow, called light streams – pink, amethyst, gold, silver, green and blue and all the hundreds of shades in between. Each light stream has a different learning pattern and this pattern takes an average of two to three hundred incarnations to fulfil. Also the Higher Self can incarnate more than one individualised soul at a time. Often in the later stages of spiritual development these souls that share a Higher Self are members of the same family.

Apparently if one could see the Higher Self one would be delighted by its great beauty. The Master has said:

'Imagine looking at a sunset, how the sky above radiates the light, how each cloud represents a facet of the pinks and oranges, the blues and greens of the sunset; and then imagine the Higher Self.

'Some may say, but if the soul has such proportions how is there room for so many in spirit? But spirit is not measured by an area of space; spirit is a dimension. It is not like your world where

you must travel from one place to another in order to experience the change of view, the different countries and the people dwelling in them. Spirit being a dimension of light contains all things in a comparatively small area in comparison to your world. Unfortunately to be able to visualise that which you have never seen is virtually impossible.'

So a true insight into the Higher Self – the total soul – can never be achieved because it is of a vastly different vibration from that of which the body is aware.

The soul has the opportunity to learn in spirit as well as upon the earth, but the earth is an important school for the soul, where the Higher Self can enrich its understanding with first-hand knowledge of the full range of human emotions. Ultimately it is where the Higher Self can come to know love. It is the planet where the soul can express itself, can move forward and has that greatest blessing of all – free will. The soul in its own environment does not have free will. It has total knowledge and understanding of life and universal law; it has accepted what it is simply to be, but that is not sufficient for truly understanding the lessons that life can offer, lessons such as compassion, tolerance, understanding and patience.

When the soul enters the physical self at the time of birth, conscious knowledge of the past is concealed. Later, at different times of life, an aspect of the Higher Self that has lived before and that has an interest or karmic investment in the particular events or lessons that are being lived through will step forward to offer help, assistance and understanding. This help is often initially recognized through synchronicity, experiences of *déjà vu* or dreaming. Through meditation and spiritual development such a link with a 'Spirit Guide' can be built upon and even parts of the past life can be recalled. The spiritually enhanced understanding of the guide can then help the individual to go forward, develop and succeed.